Trusting You Are Loved

Practices for Partnership

D1012357

Lew Epstein

In partnership with

Francine Epstein & Reppy Epstein Kirkilis

The Partnership Foundation
Mill Valley, California

Trusting You Are Loved
Practices for Partnership

Publisher's Cataloging-in-Publication Data
(Provided by Quality Books, Inc.)

Epstein, Lew, 1919–
    Trusting you are loved : practices for partnership /
 authors: Lew Epstein in partnership with Francine Epstein
 & Reppy Epstein Kirkilis.
        p. cm.
        LCCN: 98-067947
        ISBN- 0-9665919-0-9

        1. Interpersonal relations.   2. Marriage.   I. Epstein, Francine.
 II. Kirkilis, Reppy Epstein.   III. Title.
 HM132.E77 1998   158.2
                                                       QBI98-1290

Cover Design: Elizabeth Shubert
Interior Design: Cirrus Design

I dedicate this book

to

my beloved parents, Isidore and Minnie Epstein,
my sisters, Rosie, Gussie, and Ida, and my brother Jake,
whose love and kindness kept me safe.
I grew up in a family of angels.

and to

all the members of the Men's and Women's Clubs
for trusting Francine and I so fully,
and demonstrating that the practices
described in this book
can profoundly alter the quality of relationship.

Contents

Part Three—*Exercises for Partnership*

How it all began

This book has truly been created in partnership. I've had more than "a little help from my friends." This book would never have become a reality were it not for some of the extraordinary people in my life. Thank God I've learned to **let myself be loved**.

When I first discovered it was difficult for me to get everything I knew down on the written page, a special angel in my life, Jinny Ditzler, graciously honored me by offering to be my partner. She sat with me for hours, asked me questions, and listened. While I spoke she took copious notes, and while I slept she put together the makings of this book. She worked tirelessly for many months to bring it into existence. This was a supreme and selfless labor of love for which I am eternally grateful.

Then I went through a bout of cancer and radiation therapy during which time this project came to a halt.

When we were ready to tackle it again, and Jinny was in the middle of publishing her own book, *Your Best Year Yet*, our dear friend Deborah Naish agreed to become our manager and handle the book's production—a task which proved to be more far reaching than any of us imagined. We could not have done this without her.

At that point, we were fortunate enough to pass on what we had to my dearest daughter Reppy. She lovingly devoted the next nine months to writing my book, as well as adding her own immensely valuable contributions, to result in what we have today. I'm extremely proud of and grateful for the love of a daughter who would give so fully and completely to have her father's work and words expressed so beautifully into the world. She represents me. She is my heart!

As I said, this book has truly been created in partnership. Without Jinny Ditzler's gift, which breathed life into what was only a dream, this book would not have been born; without Reppy's gift, it would not have grown up to be what it is today. The love, commitment, and generosity of these women is profound.

I am forever grateful for their partnership.

Lew Epstein
September 1998

Acknowledgments from Lew and Francine

Francine and I are extremely grateful for all the love and support we have received from so many people over the last 25 years, all of which has contributed to the coming together of this book. We'd like to use this opportunity to publicly acknowledge some of them.

Our greatest fear is that we will offend someone by leaving them out. We apologize if we have omitted anyone we should have included and we are deeply sorry for the oversight. We wish we could have thanked everyone personally.

We especially want to thank our dear friends:

Lloyd Fickett, who started the first Men's Clubs for us and continued to coach us and co-create with us.

Tim Ditzler, who brought us to England and founded the London Clubs.

Joanne Black, who was the first to suggest that we work in the area of relationship between men and women, and who is a source of inspiration, coaching, and continued co-creation.

Rita Reneaux, who is a constant support and partner, and has, among other things, assisted in the design of all the courses, workshops, and retreats we've ever done. She and her husband Paul Grossman are living examples of **partnership in relationship** in action.

Other couples whose love and friendship have supported us and our work throughout the years: Helen and Stan Gold, Kathy and Charlie Smith, Peggy and Nestor Figueroa, Jinny and Tim Ditzler, and Lynne and Lloyd Fickett.

Those individuals who have gone out of their way to support us in numerous ways: Wayne Terry, Taylor Cornish, Tom Herndon, Michael Filson, Tod Zelickson, Phil Server, Grace Taylor, Patria Molé, and many, many others.

Our teacher Werner Erhard who gave us the gift of rediscovering ourselves and our own special gifts.

To our families:

Lew honors: The memory of my loving parents Minnie and Isidore Epstein, whose kindness and love live in me forever. My brother Jake, and my sisters Rosie, Gussie, and Idie, who kept me safe. My children Kenneth, Reppy, and Jonathan for always loving and forgiving me. My grandchildren Alexandra, Lorian, Peter, and Spencer, who are my inspiration for creating a world that is safe for children.

Francine honors: My mother Betty Brostoff and the memory of my father Stanley Brostoff, for bringing me up in an environment where I always knew I was loved. My brother and sister-in-law, Alan and Judy Brostoff, for their inspiration and support. My daughter Marci Levine, for her overwhelming trust, love, support, and generosity.

For the book itself: Our deepest gratitude to: Jinny Ditzler for the incredible gift of birthing the book; Paula Alter for the second draft edits; Reppy Epstein Kirkilis for putting her heart and soul into the creation of the book; Tom Marx for managing the process as liaison from our publishers, The Partnership Foundation; and Deborah Naish, whose love, commitment, intention, and perseverance allowed her to manage the entire project to completion. Our heartfelt thanks go out to all of you. We will be forever grateful.

Our deep appreciation to The Partnership Foundation for publishing this book and to all those who contributed funds toward its publication, particularly those members of the San Francisco, Phoenix, and Tucson Clubs for their generous donations. And a special, heartfelt thank you to our angels, Richard Falk, Helen and Stan Gold, and Scott Hunter.

We honor The Partnership Foundation and its commitment to bringing partnership in relationship into the world. Thank you all for loving us, forgiving us, and for letting us love you.

Acknowledgments from Reppy

Thank you, Pop, for being my teacher, my father, and my partner. It is a privilege to be your daughter, to walk beside you in this life. In the glow of your love I have discovered my path: to create safety for others, and to trust that I am loved. I am deeply honored that you have entrusted me to speak your heart and to represent your work, as well as my own, in this book. Thank you for the gift of my life, and for empowering, loving, and trusting me. I love you and celebrate you. You are truly a great man.

Thank you, Francine, for loving and taking such magnificent care of my father all these years. Your love has healed him and given him the strength to contribute to so many people. Your generosity and kindness gave our whole family a second chance. I honor and admire your wisdom, courage, brilliance, and dedication to the truth. Thank you for being my teacher.

Thank you to my wise, wonderful friends, Millie Lundrigan, Jean Bobo, and Wade Wisdom, for listening, supporting, and guiding me on this journey. I am forever blessed by your love, trust, and commitment to my growth and highest good. Thank you, dearest Deborah Naish, for being my soul mate and partner in the roller coaster ride that this book has been.

Thanks to my clients for trusting me; Wade Wisdom, for your faith and belief in who I am as a coach; my friends Alima Dieter and Cat Greenstreet, who gave me strength. I also want to thank Jinny S. Ditzler for your incredible heart, talent, commitment, huge spirit, and generosity. Your gift to all of us is immeasurable.

And to my cherished family: to my precious daughter, Alexandra, without your patience, understanding, compassion, goodness, commitment, inspiration, and integrity, I simply could not have written this book. Parenting you and learning from you is my greatest privilege. I am so proud of the fine person that you are. And to my beloved husband Johnny, thank you for making it possible for me to do my work in the world. Thank you for loving me and believing in me. Our partnership is the foundation of my life. I love you both so much!

Lew, Francine and I would also like to thank those whose good taste and commitment to excellence made an invaluable contribution to the book: editor Robin Quinn for her essential advice and commentary, as well as Jean Bobo, Kenny Epstein, Marci Levine, Tom Herndon, Dan Gurler, and Tom Marx; the entire Board of The Partnership Foundation, Elizabeth Shubert for the beautiful cover design, Chris Nolt for the gorgeous interior design, Dana Monosoff and Darren David.

I am also very grateful to everyone who has supported and sustained me, and to those who have contributed their time, expertise, and caring to shepherd this project along its way. Thank you for loving me.

Part One

The Journey Begins

CHAPTER 1

Why are we here?

This book is about how to live with other human beings. If history has proven anything, it is that we have not yet mastered our most basic challenges: first, **how to be safe with each other**, and second, **how to take care of one another**.

Why are we here? **We're here to be with people—** to learn how to communicate, have compassion, practice love and forgiveness. Since the evolution of humankind, the most fundamental dilemma plaguing us still stands: how can we, with all our diversity, fears, and seemingly insurmountable differences, live together successfully?

All of us are well aware of the monumental advances we've made in technology. We can sit at the computer in our home in Duluth and have a conversation with someone in Denmark. Fax machines, overnight mail, and cellular phones make us so much more accessible— communication seems to be at an all-time high. But are we really more connected, more intimate, safer?

As we approach the new millennium and perhaps some of the more significant challenges of our evolution, it becomes clear that in one of the most primal aspects of our existence—the way in which we relate to one another—much of the world is still in the dark ages. There is a great deal of suffering amongst us, and much of it is caused by people hurting other people, physically, emotionally, and spiritually. This global condition of disharmony, as it has been since we have walked the earth, has resulted in many of us suffering either directly or indirectly at the hands of our fellow human beings.

Thankfully, the equally common condition of striving to better our lot and promote the healing power of love, which is as old as its injurious counterpart, has resulted in many people finding ways of uplifting their lives and the lives of those around them. It's natural to want to make a positive difference—have we not all wished we could make the world a more benevolent place? We can. **We can contribute to the healing of humanity when we make the commitment to healing ourselves and others through improving the quality of our relationships.**

The journey begins with the most intimate of our relationships—the ones we have with ourselves and with our significant others. We start the process here at home and it unfolds, branching out into our workplaces and communities. While the original premise of the philosophy in this book was geared toward married men and women, virtually any two or more people—married and unmarried couples (straight or gay), family members, friends, bosses and employees, prenuptial couples, even divorced people looking for new ways to communicate and co-parent—can benefit from this work. Whether we are married or not, we are in relationship—with ourselves, and with the people in our lives.

However, since the principal intention of this book is to provide insight into what happens when two people live together in an exclusive partnership, our focus will be centered on that type of relationship.

Why be in relationship?

Most of us either are married or want to be in a committed relationship. Why? Those who are married know it's not easy—it means being constantly confronted with conflict and change. When we take on the task of sharing a lifetime with another human being, we are challenged, disappointed, frustrated, intruded upon, demanded of, misunderstood, hurt, angered, frightened. So why do we do it? Is it because we need companionship—we don't want to be alone? Well, if all we need is companionship, it would be a lot easier to just get ourselves a dog. A dog gives us the unconditional love we deserve and forgives us for everything. A dog doesn't care how we look and won't take it personally if we forget to say the instant we come home from work, *"You're the most wonderful dog I've ever known, and I thank God every day that you are in my life."*

So why, even after we've endured the pain of a divorce or been rejected or betrayed by a loved one, do we keep coming back to relationship? Because we instinctively know that being with other people is where we fulfill our true purpose on earth—to live in partnership with one another. We keep coming back because that's where our true heart's work is. After all, how can our lives be truly fulfilling if our relationships are not a source of inspiration, growth, and joy?

This book is the culmination of my life's work in the area of relationship. It is also the source document for **The Partnership Foundation,** an organization dedicated to promoting **partnership in relationship** in the world. Living according to these practices has made an immeasurable difference in the quality of my life—I only wish I had been aware of them in my younger days. On May 1, 1999, I will celebrate my eightieth birthday. I have been living and teaching this work for almost twenty-five years, and am so grateful that I can now share it with everyone.

I believe that there are basic truths and methods that foster successful relationships, and that they work with everyone from our parents to our spouse to our children to our co-workers. To be in partnership with other human beings is our consummate challenge. It's the most difficult job in the world today—it demands we bring forth the best of who we are—but the compensation for our efforts is extraordinary.

Trusting You Are Loved is about how to take on that job and discover that it can be the most rewarding and gratifying experience you've ever had. In our most intimate relationships we are asked to share our heart and soul, to risk what we have protected, to be willing to give up everything we are familiar with for the promise of what could be. That's a tall order, but as far as I'm concerned, it's the only game worth playing!

**Life can be lived in the experience
of partnership. We don't have to do it alone.
As a matter of fact, we can't. Maybe we can
survive alone, exist alone, but we can't really *live*
this life alone. Life is with people.**

Everything we do has an impact, and when we take even small steps forward in the spirit of partnership, we encourage others to do the same. When we express our basic goodness in both intimate and casual situations, we ignite a chain reaction which can invigorate another. For instance, when we're trying to pull out of a driveway during rush hour, doesn't it restore our faith in human nature when someone courteously waves to us and lets us in? We feel great and odds are we'll do it for the next person we see. On the other hand, if cars keep passing us by and no one even makes eye contact with us, it's infuriating—and we might take our impatience out on the next poor guy who wants to cut in front of us. Everything we do matters, and in these uncertain times, we have a moral responsibility to educate ourselves, actively striving to demonstrate our benevolence and nobility in every encounter.

When we create partnership, when we start from the premise that we are all one heart, the artificial boundaries that really have no place between us dissolve. In creating partnership, we are being called forth to dig deep into our souls and make healing our relationships with others our highest priority.

What is partnership in relationship?

The basic components of partnership in relationship are: **trust, honor, dignity, respect, safety, and compassionate listening.** The principles in this book come from my own experience and that of thousands of people in our Men's Clubs and Women's Clubs, as well as their families. Working together with hundreds of couples over the past twenty years, my wife Francine and I have discovered that the following ten practices can create the most powerful of partnerships:

1. **Trusting You Are Loved**
2. **Listening with Compassion**
3. **Apology**
4. **Forgiveness**
5. **Speaking from Your Heart**
6. **Creating Safety**
7. **Creating Intimacy: Include Your Partner**
8. **Handling Upsets Responsibly**
9. **Expressing Appreciation**
10. **Honoring Your Commitment**

In **Part Two**, we've devoted a chapter to each one of the above practices. In **Part Three**, you and your partner will have the opportunity to begin to explore these practices with the support of helpful reminders and exercises.

Partnership serves as the context for our relationships. When we are out of partnership, it's normal to feel resentful or distrustful, critical and angry, unloved, unappreciated, misunderstood, or frightened. When conflicts occur, we are often unable to deal with them effectively, simply because we feel that our partner is our enemy. We discover that nothing can truly be settled when we are stuck in the experience of *You against Me*. When we are returned to the experience of partnership, i.e., *You and Me united, without fault or blame, addressing whatever is causing the problem*, we find ourselves in a miraculous place where our issues, from the mundane to the monumental, have a chance to be resolved.

I believe most couples, whether they are just starting

out or have been together for many years, will find the quality of their relationships greatly enhanced as they journey together towards partnership.

Creating partnership starts with trusting I am loved

Trusting I am loved is at the heart of it all. How many of us go through life secure in the experience that we are deeply loved? Since I've spent most of my life doubting it, remembering I'm loved has been quite a struggle. Trusting I am loved is like conditioning a muscle that hasn't been used for a long time—the more it's stretched and worked, the stronger it gets.

For example, I remember a time when I was away from home on a business trip, and awoke suddenly at 3:00 AM thinking that my pillow wasn't right. Francine packs for me and knows I like my special orthopedic pillow with me all the time. I was positive this wasn't the right pillow. I imagined how she had carelessly picked up the wrong pillow and thrown it in the suitcase, thinking it wasn't that important.

The story grew and grew in my mind until I reached the ultimate stupidity—I thought: *"Why do I put up with this? I've had enough already—I'm leaving her! I'm just not going back home at the end of this trip!"* I was hurt and angry. Then I realized that I had simply forgotten that I was loved, and when I forget, I'm in pain. It brings up old wounds from the past and I become small, vengeful, petty. I knew what to do: inwardly I asked myself, *"Lewie, I know you're upset, but what's the truth? Does Francine love you?"* Of course I knew the answer—*"She loves me!"*—and a moment later, the anger disappeared and I fell immediately back to sleep. Whether or not I had the "right" pillow didn't matter any more.

It takes vigilance and discipline to train ourselves to remember the truth and let the pain go. We have all made a great investment in our particular suffering and it can be sad to say good-bye to it. It takes courage to face up to the way we are and make the choice to embrace our whole self—the greatness **and** the pettiness. Every one of us has wanted our relationships to work, and we've all done the best we could. We've meant well when it comes to making things better; however, much of the time "working on our marriage" has translated into wishing the other person were different.

We want others to change

If you ask most couples what their chief complaint is, chances are the first thing said will be: *"He doesn't..."* or *"If only she would...."* Why is it so easy to see another's faults? Why do we think **they're** the problem? Because it really looks that way to us. **It feels like the truth.** We blame our partners for the way we feel, for our frustrations, and for what we don't have in our lives. We may even be aware that we are primarily disappointed in ourselves, but since it's easier to blame someone else, we don't let our partners know that. All they see is how upset we are with them, which in turn has them get upset with us.

We don't trust that we are loved and then fault them for not loving us. We go into hiding and don't realize that we are our own worst enemy. We take ourselves away and believe they pushed us. It really seems to us that *"if only she wouldn't (fill in the blank), then I wouldn't (fill in the blank)."* We sit and stew about how right we are and about how wrong they are. We get to justify our discomfort, but find no real comfort in that. Our relationship just sits there as we tread water; gradually we get tired, and the life goes out of us.

Instead of looking at **ourselves** and owning our part in the equation, we look over **there** and immediately want the other person to be different. If they would just fix themselves, everything would be great! I believe all our suffering stems from wanting either people or circumstances to be different, or wanting ourselves to be different. I'm truly sorry, but life will always be the way it is and people will always be the way they are. Our resistance to that truth has robbed us of the true majesty and grace of being alive—it dishonors the perfection of the **way it is** and keeps us powerless to effect change.

Ask yourself this question and answer it honestly:

Has wishing that your partner would change ever made a difference? Does your judgment make things better? Does it help that you're right?

As soon as we think another person is wrong and we're right, we sit in judgment of them. In the blink of an eye, we are judge, jury, and executioner. Once we make the decision that they're to blame, we easily gather proof to support our conviction. We listen to them through the filter of condemnation. Sometimes we seem to love being right more than we love them, and are surprised when they wither before us. But we're right, right, right—**dead right!**—about what's wrong with them. Even your friends agree! It's all your partner's fault. They prove it to us over and over. *"I can't believe this! He just did it again! How much more of this can I take?"*

What we must remember is that people can't grow (or grow up) when they are being judged. Can you imagine a mother berating her toddler because he or she hasn't mastered walking? Would you put up with a teacher humiliating your child in class because the youngster's having difficulty learning fractions? Of course not. So why are we so hard on our partners? Why do we judge them so harshly and expect them to be perfect? Simple— because we are so hard on **ourselves**.

Our most fundamental relationship

The greatest opportunity in relationships is to meet ourselves. We cannot change another human being no matter how right we are. In fact, it's not really our job to work on someone else's issues, even though it can seem like a terrific idea. It is only in our relationship with ourselves that we can make changes and corrections— and yet we are so much more expert at pointing out what's wrong with someone else and giving them a little friendly advice.

Ultimately, the source of the success of our relationships with our loved ones is in **our ability to heal ourselves in the nurturing environment we and our partners create together.** In giving up the need to fix our partners, we discover who we truly are: human beings with strengths and weaknesses who are capable of manifesting profound love, compassion, forgiveness, and integrity.

It takes awareness and courage to have a successful partnership, but most of us have bought into the myth that it's supposed to be easy—**once we've found the right person.** We long for the perfection of romantic love and the bliss of living happily ever after—no wonder we're disappointed and feel like a failure when faced with the task of actually sharing life with another human being. Not to knock romantic love—it's delightful and has an important purpose: it's crucial in bringing people together so that they recognize their connection and make a commitment. However, it's not designed to sustain a lifetime of changes and conflicts.

Very few of us learned the ways of partnership in our early lives. We all want and deserve love, but don't have the tools necessary to sustain a long-term relationship. So when the honeymoon is over, it's a lot easier to blame the other person. Blame comes naturally to us—it takes no effort:

- "It's **her** fault."
- "**He** made me feel this way."
- "Everything was fine until **she** started doing that."
- "The only reason I yell is because **he** won't listen."

We think we know best

Because we are human, most of us believe that things should be the way **we** want them to be. We think we should be a particular way and so should our partners. It's easy to invalidate what we don't like—it's much harder to look beyond the surface to the hidden potential of a situation. We think we or our partners need to change and improve—sometimes drastically.

Let's give ourselves a break here—we don't have to be perfect to be happy! We actually can't grow significantly or help another to grow until we can **be okay with the way we are**. Just as we can't shame the toddler into walking, we also can't beat ourselves into being better people. And yet we try to do that all the time—how hard we are on ourselves! The more defective we think we are, the less we are able to heal and move forward. It's such exhausting work, and so futile.

And by the way, what **is** a better person? One with no jealousy, fear, arrogance, anger, or pain? There is no such person—and that's not what we should be wasting our time striving for. We are human. It's a package deal—we get all of it—the serenity and the suffering, the confusion and the caring, the love and the loneliness. Let's stop trying to be different and embrace who we are. We're okay—it's time to stop repairing what isn't broken.

How can we make our relationships work?

This book is about discovering how to be an appropriate human being. The American Heritage dictionary defines **appropriate** as: *Suitable for a particular person, condition, occasion, or place; fitting*. Being appropriate doesn't mean being right, perfect, or flawless. It means having the ability to be flexible, to learn—we're willing to do what needs to be done. The key word here is **willingness**. It is through our willingness to discover what's appropriate that we'll find our way. And how do we learn to be appropriate? Well, how does the toddler learn to walk? He falls down a lot. To discover how to be appropriate in life, we must go through being inappropriate. And since we are so hard on ourselves, we must strive to develop a kind and patient attitude as we stumble through our awkward periods and learn our life lessons.

So how can we begin to make our relationship work? I suggest trying on the following premise:

Imagine that every time you talk to your partner, you're actually talking to yourself.

Just ponder that for a moment. How would you speak to another human being if they were **you**? We all know how sensitive we are to an impatient, critical tone of voice. We know how it feels when someone is condescending or accuses us falsely. Think back on a recent interaction with your partner where something you said upset them. Now try to imagine if you had been the one on the receiving end of that communication. How did it feel? Could it have been said a little more kindly? Would you want an apology? How would you like to be spoken to?

I've learned an important truth in my life: **I often treat others the way I treat myself**. When I'm impatient with myself, I'll be impatient with you. When I'm criticizing myself, I'm more likely to criticize you. When I feel loving toward me, I'll feel loving toward you. I'm always the source—always at the heart of it.

Relationships start to work when we stop pointing the finger at our partners, demanding, whether blatantly or covertly, *"When are you going to shape up?"* What if your partner said this to you? Would you immediately snap to attention, bow, and say, *"Whatever you say, your Highness!"*? Of course not. You'd probably say something more like: *"Oh, yeah? And when are **you** going to shape up?"*

It's time to stop pointing the finger in the other direction. I remember an old saying from my childhood: when you're pointing the finger at someone, there are three fingers pointing back at you. Let's train ourselves to be responsible for what we're bringing to the party. However, this doesn't mean we now get to blame ourselves and think everything is **our** fault. The truth is, no one is to blame! Blame is useless! All it does is make some people right and others wrong—that's its only purpose.

Judgment is a given

So what does this all mean? Simply that judgment and condemnation have no useful or redeeming qualities—**ever**. Now, this doesn't mean that we can become completely nonjudgmental—we probably can't, not in this lifetime. Human beings judge—it's as natural as breathing. We may not be able to stop judging completely, but we **can** change the way we relate to our judgments.

For instance, we can become **aware** that we are judging and of the pain that it causes. We can also let go of our self-righteousness: *"I'm judging you right now and I'm sorry. I know it hurts you when I think I'm right and you're wrong."* We can become responsible for the impact our judgments have on our loved ones and ourselves. And we can learn how to become aware of the judgments while we're having them, realize that they are only opinions, look them squarely in the eye and say, *"No, thanks!"*

Sometimes what we judge most about our partners is what we judge in ourselves—the way our partner acts reminds us of our own shortcomings. Being close with another person can be like looking in the mirror and constantly noticing all the flaws and imperfections.

We have little tolerance for our partner's behavior because it's too familiar. We can't stand seeing our own weaknesses manifested in living color by the very person we hoped would solve all our problems. How disappointing! How dare they be so human! In relationship, the best of us and the worst of us are right there in front of us, all the time. How we see our partner starts with how we see ourselves.

Why create partnership?

When we're partners in a thriving business, we have a common goal and work at it together, providing a multitude of services for one another:

- **Respecting the differences and honoring each other's contributions**

- **Listening effectively and brainstorming for solutions**

- **Honestly pointing out mistakes**

- **Forgiving and being patient**

- **Teaching and supporting**

- **Remaining committed during the tough times**

Couples who skate in competitions (such as the Olympics) demonstrate the kind of partnership we often dream about. Focused, determined, and single-minded, they look out for one another every second, knowing that their triumph depends ultimately on how well they take care of each other. Isn't it interesting that we often don't think and act this way at home with the people we love the most?

Instead we might have the thought: *"Now I'm home, I can be myself, stop having to keep my act together, and finally let my hair down!"* There's nothing wrong with having those thoughts, except that frequently we unleash the worst of ourselves on our innocent families. Tired, stressed, and irritable, we forget our responsibility to our loved ones and take out our frustrations on them.

During a meeting at one of our Men's and Women's Clubs, a couple shared about how they got into trouble in the first year of their marriage. They were both having a lot of success getting their businesses going, but things stopped being so great at home. Before their wedding, they took exquisite care of each other—talking, listening, playing, sharing their visions, supporting one another's goals. But after they were married, they would collapse in their chairs when they got home at night and say, *"Thank goodness that's over, I'm exhausted!"* Their workday was finished, so they both expected to come home and be nurtured and rejuvenated by the other. Instead of feeling loved and supported, they were continually disappointed and became resentful. Neither one was being responsible for the well-being of their relationship—like so many of us, they took it for granted, hoping the other person would make it fun again.

Fortunately, they soon became aware of the dynamic, forgave one another, and created a new context for their relationship:

The Front Door isn't the Finish Line!

The work isn't over once we've said, *"I do."* Unlike fairy tales, where all the troubles occur during the story and end with a blissful marriage, making a commitment to a relationship is actually the beginning of our adventure. Our most significant challenges are yet to come, but so are our greatest rewards.

We are all capable of having our relationships succeed—the wisdom of the ages belongs to us and lives inside our hearts. It begins with trusting we are loved and our willingness to let go of negative judgments and assessments about our partners and ourselves. It's time to realize that the situation between us and our partner is nobody's fault—it actually **needs to be the way it is** so that we can do our necessary healing work during this lifetime.

Nothing is wrong

Imagine for a moment that there is nothing wrong with you, your partner, or the relationship. You are both responsible for the way it is, but neither one of you is **wrong**. Let your partner off the hook, and yourself! Put down that heavy load and stop invalidating everything that doesn't fit the illusion of the perfect life. What would it feel like if you could have faith that your relationship was evolving exactly as it should, knowing in your heart that by letting go of judgment, the path you needed to take would become clear?

Try on the notion that you and your partner have everything it takes to make your relationship work. Neither one of you is inherently insufficient; however, you probably could use some helpful information. Would you be able to perform a successful liver transplant this afternoon if you were asked—even if you really wanted to? Would you think something was wrong with you because you couldn't? Most of us think somehow we should already have our doctorate degree from the School of Relationship, even when we've been given so little training.

You're reading this book, so you already are interested in improving your skills. Go easy on yourself, my friend—you're a courageous, noble being who needs a few pointers. Healing your relationship with your partner is God's work. It's not a burden—it's actually an opportunity that should be welcomed.

And what an opportunity!

In partnership, we can grow up together. We can let go of the pain of our past, creating the future in a safe environment where there's room to make mistakes and learn. Much of becoming the best person we can be is available in the singular experience of two human beings who love one another.

You and I are here to realize we are One—that this life experience is universal. We have the chance to end the myth of separation through the reconnection of our hearts.

Why are we here? To create partnership. As fellow travelers on a common voyage, our purpose is clear, our task most sacred. We can celebrate the opportunity to reclaim a quality of relationship that is the birthright of all people. It is my privilege and honor to offer this book to you and your loved ones as part of your healing experience. I thank God for people such as yourself who are willing to have their lives represent the dignity of one human being striving for the glory of all humanity. Thank you for your courage, and bless you on your journey towards partnership in relationship.

CHAPTER 2

The Circle of Partnership

When do we learn to be in relationship?

Something vital was missing from my education: **what I needed to know to be a successful human being amongst other human beings.** How many of us feel our education provided that? Between the rules of grammar and the mathematical formulas, where was the teaching about human values? Where's the school that creates a safe environment for us to explore who we truly are, that teaches us to trust that we are loved, that encourages us to honor the people in our lives? Sadly, in many of our schools today, there is more violence and fear than education—children aren't even able to learn about the basic goodness of life, much less their ABCs.

But occasionally I find something that gives me hope. Over the years I have had the privilege of visiting the Waldorf School my granddaughter Alexandra attends. There is an experience of safety and harmony there that I never knew in my childhood. The students learn not only academics and practical skills, but also how to respect, appreciate, and value one another. I was deeply moved by the bond the children have with their classmates and teachers—they're all learning and growing up together.

How well I remember my first day of school! I held my mother's hand as we walked down the strange streets until we came to the gate. I was so frightened—the playground was full of rowdy children I'd never seen before. I eventually made friends, but never really felt comfortable—over the years I hid in books and tried to cope as best I could. But I never let down my guard, and I didn't learn anything about other people except that in order to exist, I had to make sure they never saw how afraid I was.

So where do we learn how to be with another human being? In our families? Most of us just learned how to survive there too. Our parents were busy dealing with their own fears and problems—how could they teach us what they could not live themselves? So when do we find out what it takes to have successful relationships? In college? When we land our first jobs? When we get married?

Learning as we go

Learning how to be in relationship with other people is the ultimate on-the-job training. As children, our role models were our parents and other people who were doing the best they could with what they had learned from **their** parents. We were often isolated in our childhood homes, coping with the day-to-day struggles of our particular family dynamic, then we were thrust into the world to fend for ourselves and (hopefully) figure out how to grow up. We've all done amazingly well, considering, but many of us are still struggling on some level with what it takes to have a truly successful, fulfilling relationship with another person.

How I got here

In my marriage to my first wife Norma, I was constantly afraid. Afraid of not being a good husband, father, or provider. I felt inadequate and insecure and took it all out on my family—they never knew when I was going to get angry and criticize them. They lived in fear of me, and I of them. There was a lot of love in our family, but very little emotional safety. No one felt known, listened to, or appreciated. I always thought it was all my fault, until I discovered that almost everyone else I knew lived in a similar situation. It was the typical American middle-class family—people who loved one another but were unable to take care of themselves or each other. Because we were in pain, we hurt one another all the time.

After twenty-six years of marriage, Norma and I got a divorce. It was a terrible time for all of us—I felt like such a failure. It wasn't that Norma and I didn't love each other, but living together had become unbearable. After we separated, I wondered if I would ever have the kind of relationship I dreamed of. And then I met Francine.

It was in the loving support of this relationship that Francine and I discovered we had much to learn about how to live with another person. The difference was, we were determined to find out—committed to making our marriage last. Over the years, we became involved in extensively training ourselves to become successful partners. With the help and dedication of many friends, our family, and Men's and Women's Club members, we have discovered some simple truths about how to make relationships work, and how to create **partnership**—what we consider to be the highest level of relationship.

As we begin this conversation about partnership, let's look at its opposite. When we get into destructive patterns in our relationships, we find ourselves in an **adversarial** situation—our partner feels like the enemy. We get stuck on a treadmill of expectations, disappointments, withheld communications, and resentment. We've all been there—for some of us, it's the condition we're most familiar with.

The Destructive Cycle of Relationship

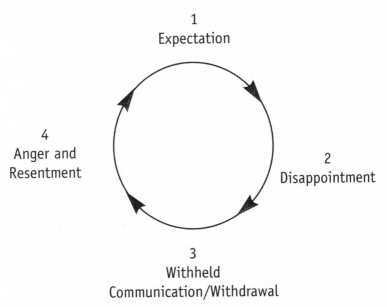

1
Expectation

4
Anger and
Resentment

2
Disappointment

3
Withheld
Communication/Withdrawal

This is a diagram of what we experience in our adversarial relationships. Some of us never get off this track—we get stalled at anger and resentment, and stop.

Nothing gets resolved; we just learn to cope, shove it under the rug, and keep going. The expectations begin, the cycle starts anew—but we end up in the same old place.

1. **EXPECTATION:** *To look forward to the likely occurrence or appearance of something; anticipation, hoping, waiting.*

We have expectations all the time—we can't help it. Mischief is created, however, when we **expect** our expectations to come true. Our hopes and dreams tend to be grandiose, absolute, far-reaching, and iron-clad; we often feel cheated and betrayed if we don't get what we want. This is understandable when we look at some of the prevailing myths of our society. From fairy tales and classic literature to romance novels and Hollywood, we've been handed a false bill of goods about ecstatic couples in effortless relationships. We've been looking for the happy ending—whatever that may mean to us.

However, in real life, there is no ending—there is only **process**. Even though we know that kind of idealized relationship isn't realistic, sometimes our hearts still hold out for it—expecting, hoping, dreaming. No wonder we often feel let down by our real-life relationships, jobs, families, friends. Our expectations, fueled by both the culture and our inner wishes, become a trap into which we fall, unable to honor and appreciate what we have.

And when it comes to relationships, our expectations may start long before we even meet our partner. When we're imagining what might be in store, we think:

- *"I'll be loved unconditionally and they'll never get upset with me."*
- *"I won't need anyone else—they'll fulfill all my needs."*
- *"When I find the right person, I'll finally be happy. I'll never be lonely again."*
- *"After I meet my true love, all my problems will be solved."*

Many of us spend our days in a constant state of hoping and anticipating, so we end up being crestfallen much of the time. Often we don't realize we've even had an expectation until it isn't met and we are disappointed.

2. DISAPPOINTMENT: *To be frustrated or thwarted by the failure to satisfy a hope, desire, or expectation.*

When real life doesn't fit our mold, we're frequently—and understandably—disappointed. Our first thought often is: *"There's something wrong, it shouldn't be this way."*

In any given situation we're anticipating, it's natural to imagine how it will turn out—but human beings do more than that. We make up the scenario, wanting to believe we have control over the outcome, then get upset when it doesn't go according to plan. I believe we need to trust that whatever is happening in our lives is there for a purpose: to teach us something. If we can stop invalidating what's going on, then we can be present to the gifts it holds for us.

Disappointments are commonplace when we live with another human being:

- **You call him after an upsetting conversation with the auto mechanic, but he just gives you advice about**

how you should have handled
it differently.

- You come home after a hard day at the
office wanting understanding, but all she
can do is complain about *her* hard day—
at the office or at home with
the children.

- You want him to assert himself sexually
the way he did when you were first
dating, but he's always too tired and
self-absorbed.

- You wish she would notice how much
you've been doing around the house, but
she seems to take it for granted.

People hardly ever act the way we want them to.
When I ask, *"How would you like your partner to act?"* often
I hear, *"More like me!"*

After being disappointed over and over and not
feeling like we can do anything about it, we often become
resigned and stop communicating. *"Why bother? He
doesn't care about me anyway—if he did, he'd notice how
gloomy I've been and say something. Why should I always be
the one to bring things up?"* Our disappointments add up
over time, just a penny's worth at first, but accumulating
until we've got quite an inventory. We don't tell our
partners how we feel anymore—why should we?—they
just get upset. But the more we hide, the more we
suffer. We stop communicating and withdraw, taking
ourselves away.

3. WITHHELD COMMUNICATION AND WITHDRAWAL:
WITHHOLD—*To keep in check; restrain. To refrain
from giving, granting, or permitting.* WITHDRAW—*To*

take back or away; remove. To retreat, retire, become detached.

Remember when you and your partner were first together?—there was always so much to talk about! You'd notice older couples in restaurants staring out the window or silently eating their meals—barely speaking at all—and vow you'd never end up like that. Early on, it was easy to tell the truth and be heard, and you promised each other to always say how you really felt and ask for what you wanted.

So what happened? For most of us, telling the truth became dangerous. When we said how we felt, we were misunderstood, accused, criticized. Telling the truth stopped looking like such a good idea—it looked safer and more reasonable to just hold onto our disappointments and fears than take the risk to share them. So we gradually took ourselves away, closed down, and withdrew.

At this point we start doing everything from hanging up on each other to walking out the door, to responding in monosyllabic grunts, or quietly avoiding each other in martyred silence. We may even realize that the only way to move beyond our destructive patterns is to communicate, but our fear keeps us hidden, paralyzed, unable to reach out. Such pain we feel when we take ourselves away!—it hurts us and our partners so much when we withdraw our love.

We're suffering, but we don't dare speak. Our partners may not even know why we're upset and feel powerless—perhaps blaming themselves or not knowing how to break down the wall. After a while, they withdraw too—no longer willing to risk rejection. The atmosphere becomes stifling—two people merely existing like estranged roommates, fearful and resigned in private worlds, unable to stop the downward spiral.

4. ANGER AND RESENTMENT: ANGER—*Intense displeasure or hostility.* RESENTMENT—*Indignation or ill will as a result of a real or imagined grievance.*

Often the hidden hurts smolder over time, finally exploding in a torrent of red-hot anger and resentment. Our cups runneth over and we lash out—at last speaking the truth but in so much pain that we want to hurt the other person as much as possible—we want them to suffer the way we've suffered. It's in this state that we are often out of control and even verbally abusive—screaming, accusing, hurling insults, making generalizations starting with such phrases as: *"You never..., you always..., you can't... , you won't...."* Underneath this tirade, we are desperately crying out to be heard, but our partners can barely listen since they're feeling so viciously attacked.

What do we do in the presence of this kind of emotion? Most often, we defend ourselves: justify our actions, explain why, push the blame back on them, even retaliate with our own offense—anything to protect ourselves from the onslaught.

If someone isn't able to diffuse the anger, it can escalate to a point where both people are terrified—afraid of their own emotions, the feelings of the other, of what's being said, and of the possibility that they won't be able to recover from it. Our words are flying out of control, our hearts are racing—and it looks as if this may be the end of the relationship. How frightening—how painful to feel the person we love the most has become an enemy—our opponent!

The endless cycle

Hopefully, in the midst of this, we won't walk out on each other and end the relationship. Time goes by, the heat of anger cools, and we start to think things will get better:

- *"Maybe someday he'll realize I'm right."*
- *"I'll just give her some space and she'll come around."*
- *"I hope he realizes how much he's hurt me and apologizes."*
- *"I'll back off and she'll come to her senses."*

The expectations start again—we hope that something (i.e., **they**) will change and that the problems will disappear.

Here's a definition I like: **Insanity is continuing to do something the same way and expecting a different result.** It certainly holds true in relationships—if we keep doing it the way we've always done it and expect it to turn out differently, we will be profoundly disappointed—yet that's what we often do. Until we get off the treadmill and try something new, we will always end up back where we started—and wonder why!

If we stay on this destructive cycle, we usually end up in one of two places: physically separated from our partners, or "stuck" with them—resigned, hopeless, bitter, our hearts dead, our lives an endless chain of uncommunicated hurts and unresolved conflicts.

There is another way. Once we can break free of the loop and move forward, we will find ourselves on a very different path. On this path, we can work through any issue in our relationships and use it to strengthen and empower ourselves and our partners. In my life, partnership has been the road map to a place where I have finally become the person I always wanted to be.

The Circle of Partnership

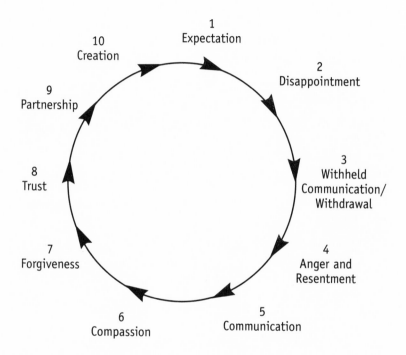

Communication is the key

We know in our hearts that nothing ever really gets resolved when we stop talking to one another. Alone in our private anguish, the hurts and resentments only seem to gather weight and mass as we nurse them over time. **In relationship, ultimately it's not the communicating that kills us—it's the lack of it.**

We all know that we should try to talk things out, but when we do, we often get even more upset. Why? Because our communications tend to be judgments, assessments, rationalizations, or attacks. We communicate, but we end up accusing, fighting, and arguing—and all this does is keep us on the destructive cycle.

The kind of communication we will be exploring in this book takes you on a different course and onto a different, positive circle. Once we get off that destructive carousel, our communications lead us to an experience of **compassion**, **forgiveness**, and **trust**. When we are in **partnership**, we can **create** anything together and resolve even the most difficult conflicts. This book will serve as a guide to mastering the productive parts of the cycle—assisting you and your partner as you move forward.

Here we go again!

The interesting thing to observe about the **Circle of Partnership** is that you'll notice the **Destructive Cycle of Relationship** is a part of it—they're not two separate entities. When we get past No. 4, **Anger and Resentment**, and move on to No. 5, **Communication**, eventually progressing to No. 10, **Creation**—what a relief! It's a cause for celebration—but what happens then? Do we all go to The Land of No Problems and live happily ever after? We may feel great—our partnership has been restored and all is well. In this state of new-found bliss, we might say to ourselves:

"It feels so good now—I'll never be disappointed again! I'll never withhold or let myself get so resigned that I don't communicate. From now on, things will be different. As of this

moment, we're not going to make the same mistakes—this is a new beginning!"

Sound familiar? Well, look where we are—we're back at No. I—**Expectation**. The cycle begins anew! We're human beings—we live in expectation. We can't avoid going back to the beginning. It's the Law of the Universe, and it exists because we are always growing, evolving, and striving to meet our challenges. It's nature's way to keep moving us around the wheel—how else will we master it?

The majesty of partnership is that it provides us with tools that support us in getting out of the destructive loop, using each conflict instead as a springboard to healing. Each time we find ourselves upset with our partners, it is an opportunity to discover the next truth about ourselves—and in doing so, we can strengthen the very core of our relationship.

The Practices of Partnership

In Part Two, we present the **Practices of Partnership**. Some of them are distinct and linear, others are inclusive and overlap. All are designed to be used in unison with each other in a harmonious rhythm, and as such, they come together as a path for living life. These practices are synergistic and give life to one another—just as we do when we stop being adversaries and realize that we've always been on the same side. To be in partnership means to go back to our roots—it is the foundation of who we are.

We don't have to do this alone—we can't do this alone. As human beings, we have the innate ability to awaken again and again from our slumber to bring forth the promise of our very existence: to live in peace with one another. The dignity of our true nature is waiting to be reclaimed as we embark upon this most exhilarating adventure of living with another human being.

Part Two

Practices for Partnership

CHAPTER 1

Trusting You Are Loved

*If you want to honor the people
you love, let them love you.*

You are already loved

I have good news. You are loved—the people in your life already love you. Your partner, parents, brothers, sisters, friends and family all love you. But if you're like many of us, deep down you may not believe it. You question it, try to get proof, doubt, test—hoping to play your cards right so that people will love you. Guess what? They already do. You don't have to do anything to **get** their love—you **have** it. Imagine for a moment how different your life would be if you really **trusted** you were loved.

We think we know what it's like to be loved. We think we know how people would act if they **really** loved us. We think real love has to be demonstrated in a certain way—*"Prove it to me! Show me!"* So what happens? People don't act the way we want them to act and we're disappointed. *"They wouldn't treat me like that if they loved me." "He wouldn't say that if he loved me." "If she really loved me,*

she wouldn't get angry." Sound familiar? We all do this—
it's as if we have a voice-over recording running in our
heads all the time, pointing out the evidence that we're
not loved—and as we all know, we can always find
evidence if we look for it!

We all have our own special list supporting the
notion that we're not loved. After all, if people **really**
loved us, they wouldn't:

- **Disagree with us**
- **Judge, blame, or criticize us**
- **Continue to do things that always upset us**
- **Refuse to give us what we want**
- **Nag, complain, or get angry**
- **Falsely accuse or misunderstand us**
- **Make emotional demands**
- **Resent us or hold grudges**
- **and on and on . . .**

When we're not trusting we are loved, everything
that happens or doesn't happen only makes our case
stronger. After a lifetime of doubting and years and years
of collecting "conclusive" data, it's no wonder that we
have trouble letting ourselves be loved. So what happens
when someone tries to love us?

**Even if they express their love, we can't fully accept
it. We aren't able to hear them because their
message contradicts our belief that *we are not
loved*. Sometimes, if our partners become
too frustrated trying to love us, they may
give up—and we'll end up with the
empty comfort of *being right*.**

I remember a Club member telling me that she used to tally up all the loving things her partner did so that she could convince herself she was loved. Unfortunately, she also had a mental list of all the "unloving" things, too—and because she didn't trust, no matter how much her partner loved her, she could never quite believe it. The "unloving'" list won out every time. When we're not trusting we are loved, no amount of reassurance will ever be enough to convince us.

Not trusting we're loved starts early

When I was very young, I believed that in order to be loved I had to be perfect and please everyone. I'd say, *"Don't worry. I'll always love you. I'm here for you."* But what was I really saying? It was: *"If I love you, will you love me? If I'm here for you, will you be there for me?"*

When I began to get successful in acting and public speaking, I felt more secure. But what I really craved was the attention and approval I received, and like so many of us, **I thought attention was love**. So I still wasn't satisfied. The adoration I got when I was on stage was fleeting, and I then had to go home and face my fears with the real people in my life. I also discovered that being popular was different from being loved. Many times, when we finally get the attention we think we want, it can become a tremendous intrusion. We may find ourselves thinking:

- *"Leave me alone!"*
- *"Can't I have a moment's peace?"*
- *"What do you want **now**?"*
- *"Don't bother me!"*

- *"Why are you always asking me questions?"*
- *"Give me some space—you're suffocating me!"*

We say we want people to love us, and when they do, we don't let them, or criticize the way they do it. We want attention and get it, then reject it, and subsequently fault the people around us for not really loving us! Aren't we crazy? Aren't we human!

When we're children, we take everything personally. How can we not? We want our parents' approval more than anything, and when we displease or disappoint them, we think there's something wrong with **us**. How many of our parents were able to express anger without rejecting us or withdrawing their love? They tried to offer guidance, but when they'd correct us, we thought it was because we weren't good enough. That makes sense, since most of us didn't have parents who were able to correct without judgment. We grew up thinking we had to act a certain way to be loved, and our lives were spent pursuing something we already had.

I've seen the transformation in people when they realize their parents always loved them, realize that the intolerance they may have experienced as children was only a reflection of the pain **their parents felt about themselves**—it had nothing to do with whether or not they themselves were deeply loved. They cry tears of release and let go of so many burdens. We've all wasted energy and time trying to get people to love us. If we could only stop long enough to see that they already do.

Several years ago, I was in Washington, DC speaking to a group of parents and their teenagers. At the beginning of the meeting, I said, *"I notice how many of the teens seem to be holding back. How many of you didn't want to come here? How many of you feel you were dragged here by your parents?"* Nearly all the young people raised their hands.

I decided to start the meeting by telling them I wanted to speak to their parents on their behalf. I said to the parents—*"This is what your child wants to say to you."*

"Mom and Dad, I want you to know that I don't feel heard. I don't feel included. I don't feel appreciated and I feel strongly that too much is expected of me. I feel like I can't win and that I can't do anything right."

Most of the teens got excited, saying, *"Yes, yes, that's exactly how I feel!"*

And then I said to them, I want to speak to you on behalf of your parents. I said to the teenagers—*"This is what your parents want to say to you."*

"We want you to know that we don't feel heard. We don't feel included. We don't feel appreciated and we feel strongly that too much is expected of us. We feel like we can't win and that we can't do anything right."

The parents and children looked at each other in astonishment. Then they all fell into each others' arms. In relationship, the complaints we have are often the same as our loved one's. The statement, *"You don't listen to me!"* is often followed by the response, *"Well, you don't listen to me, either!"* Trusting we are loved begins when we remember that we don't have to go looking for the love we never lost in the first place. We are all one heart.

We forgot that we are loved

We've gotten in the habit of wishing people and circumstances were different, and we've forgotten that we are loved. Somewhere in the past we knew it, and at some point we forgot. It's as simple and as complicated as that. If we are convinced we are not loved, the people who love us don't stand a chance. They can't say *"I love you"* enough—if they say it a million times we'll wonder why they didn't say it a million and one times. We'll see whatever happens through the filter of *"I'm not loved."*

As infants, most of our needs are met, usually without hesitation. We're cuddled, fed, pampered, and adored. But one day—and this is inevitable—when we cry out, Mama doesn't come right away (of course, we can't know that she's in the bathroom with an upset stomach), or when she speaks to us, her voice isn't soothing (how can we understand that she just had an argument with our father?), and we feel frightened. As we get older, more and more of these moments occur, and our sense of safety is threatened.

How are we to possibly know that this is just the way life is, that we don't have to take it personally? Sadly, most of us don't understand that, so we make decisions in the most tender recesses of our hearts that color the rest of our lives. We keep searching for the time when all our needs were met and we didn't have to worry—trying to find that place, longing and grieving for it.

Eventually most of us get married, hoping our partners will provide that womb-like retreat from the cares of life, and are again disappointed—because, most likely, they're hoping to get the same thing from us! But we forget the most important truth—that Mama didn't ever stop loving us, even though sometimes she was tired and overwhelmed. Daddy always loved us—even when he was angry and wouldn't listen. It's true—we are loved! We can stop searching for the sunken treasure, because it's right here, glowing and sparkling before us.

We hurt our loved ones when we don't let them love us

Sometimes there is a high price to pay for not trusting—we damage our relationships because we're convinced we're not loved. We drive our partners crazy trying to make sure they love us when they already do. When we won't let ourselves be loved, we're a bottomless pit—no matter how much reassurance we get, we always need more. We also tend to distance ourselves from people when we don't believe we are deserving of their love—it's a form of protection. How does it feel when we offer ourselves to someone but they reject us because **they** feel unworthy? It's painful, and we'll probably think twice about offering ourselves to them again.

Eventually, if we're so positive our partners don't love us, we can actually push them away permanently. It's one of life's little ironies: we say we want to be loved, but since our partners can never love us "just the right way," we're constantly resentful and end up accusing them of not really loving us! After awhile, they may feel they can't win. Their real (but imperfect, human) love is helpless in the face of our conviction that we are not worthy. And the more love we want, the more we complain that they're not giving it to us. So they leave, and we get to be right. *"See, I told you that he didn't really love me!"*

Yes, I know you can give me chapter and verse to prove that he doesn't love you. Yes, I know she can be terrible when she's upset. It's true—you've both put up with so much. But why hold onto that history? Why keep telling the same story over and over again—what good does it do?

Let's start with this: Most of us don't know how to **let ourselves be loved**. Why don't we stop blaming our partners for not loving us enough? Our partners are doing the best they can. Let's become aware of how we let all the wonderful things they do slip by, how we focus on all the things we don't like. Let's stop making them the bad guys and realize that **we** have something to do with the fact that **we don't trust that we are loved.**

I feel safe in the presence of people who I trust love me and let me love them. I can be myself, I don't have to pretend. At times I can be childish, angry, obstinate, lovable, forgiving, compassionate—I can share my feelings or I can be silent. I can be myself when I'm with people who let me love them, and I can speak truthfully, from my heart. We've always been told the greatest gift we can give another is to love them. This surely is important, but I think that an even greater gift is letting **ourselves** be loved.

The journey of love

Trusting that we're loved involves the highest state of consciousness and awareness. But how does love, as a journey, begin? As infants, we **need** love for our very survival. As we grow and develop, the way we are loved changes too. Here's the progression:

1. **Needing** to be loved
2. **Wanting** to be loved
3. **Letting** yourself be loved
4. **Listening** you are loved
5. **Trusting** you are loved

As I mentioned earlier, at some point in our childhood we become afraid and begin doubting we are loved. That's when we start **wanting** to be loved. It's okay to

want to be loved and this is part of the process, but it is a
desire, a desire often based on an assumption—**I am not
loved**. Many of us never move beyond that point. We
spend our whole lives in a state of wanting that which we
already possess. To move from wanting to letting
ourselves be loved can take only a moment—it starts
with our willingness to allow the already existing love
"permission" to enter.

In this journey, we move toward trusting we are
loved—but even that in itself is not a destination we
arrive at and never leave. We are constantly moving back
and forth from port to port as we heal, and we'll find
ourselves coming home to trusting we are loved more
quickly and easily as we grow. **Trusting we are loved** is
an umbrella which encompasses **listening we are loved**
and **letting ourselves be loved**—they are all distinct
levels of the same experience.

What does it mean to let ourselves be loved?

Quite a few years ago, I was getting ready to go to a
Men's Club meeting. Just before I left, Francine affection-
ately patted my hair. It is one of those little things she
does to show her love, but it used to really annoy me. I
would shrink from her touch, irritated, and think:

"Leave me alone—stop pawing me!" or

*"What's wrong with my hair? Why do you always have
to do something to my hair?"*

But this time, I didn't pull back. I let her pet me the way
she wanted, and I enjoyed it. In that moment, I was
surrounded by the presence of her love and the amaze-
ment of not having had my knee-jerk reaction. I could

feel her pride and joy in sending me out into the world to do my work. It had been so simple—and yet one of the hardest things I had ever accomplished. **I had let her love me**.

When I got to the Club meeting, I shared this story with the men—what a conversation we had that night! So many admitted having the same reactions—rejecting their wife's touch, feeling intruded upon when their wives wanted affection, resenting the demands put on them for intimacy. We marveled at how human we all were: complaining about how much we wanted intimacy and yet often refusing it.

During the course of the evening, many of the men realized they were not letting themselves be loved and made plans to go home and apologize. I believe that one of the main reasons women wither away in relationships is because all they want to do is love their men, but the men won't let them. It's so difficult for us to be loved, stroked, paid attention to—it's embarrassing and we don't think we deserve it. We have a hard time just accepting it for what it is—an expression of appreciation.

When men are not trusting they are loved, much of the time they hear their partner's requests or statements as criticism. For instance:

"Why are you wearing that tie?" is no longer a simple question. We misinterpret the message, thinking it means:

"You're a tasteless boor!" or

"I know what's best." or

"There's something wrong with you."

Even though there may be some judgment in that question, we forget to look beyond it to what she is also saying: *"She loves me. She just wants me to look and feel good."*

Of course, this goes both ways—when a woman doesn't trust that she's loved, she may need to be constantly reassured, but sooner or later her partner will do the "wrong" thing and her confidence collapses. She may pick at him constantly, questioning what he's doing and why. Having to work late at the office means he doesn't like spending time at home (with her!). Wanting to play golf with friends means that he would go to any lengths to avoid contact.

Men often feel there's nothing they can do to convince women that they are loved. They blame themselves for their wife's unhappiness, which makes them even more distant and unable to connect—and the vicious circle continues. We need to become aware of the impact we have when we don't let our partners love us. It's not bad, it's just human—but like so many other common behaviors, it has its cost. It's time to train ourselves to break free of the habit of listening to our partners as if we are not loved. We need to learn to **listen we are loved.**

How can I listen that I'm loved?

The definition of **listen** is: ***To make an effort to hear something; to pay attention, heed***. What would it be like if we made an effort to hear that we were loved when our partner spoke to us?

If our partner says, *"Take your jacket, it's cold,"* we might want to react by saying sarcastically, *"Hey, I'm not a child! Don't you think I know when I need a jacket?"* But if we **listen**, we will hear something completely different: *"Honey, it's cold today and I want you to be warm. There's a flu bug going around and I'm concerned about your health.*

I love you." That's what we hear when we **listen that we're loved.**

It takes practice, and it's not always easy, but there's another way to react when your partner says, *"Take your jacket."* You could say, *"Thank you for loving me and being concerned about me, but I'm not going to be outside that long and I don't want to carry something else around all day."* You could thank your partner for loving you. You could speak the way you'd want your partner to speak to you. Besides—when you listen that you're loved, you may realize they're right—so for heaven's sake, take the jacket!

We may hear the words, but we don't really *listen.*

We hear the words but we miss the message: *"I love you."* Practice imagining they're saying what they say because they love you. Do it for the next three things your partner says. Instead of adding to the case that you're not loved, try saying to yourself: *"He loves me." "She loves me!"* If he says, *"When are you going to talk to your boss about that problem you're having?"* He loves me! If she says, *"I can't believe you stayed up late again working! Don't you know you're going to get sick if you keep this up?"* She loves me! When we **listen** we are loved, we're **letting** ourselves be loved, and our perceptions can alter completely.

When is it most difficult to listen we are loved? When we think we're not worthy of being loved, of course. What if our self-esteem is shaky and we're often incredibly harsh on ourselves? Why do we forgive another for some small infraction—and then spend two months beating ourselves over the head for doing the very same thing? As harshly as we judge others, we judge ourselves even more—we know exactly where to twist the knife.

Even the people we are closest to don't know our vulnerabilities they way we do—or exploit them with such ease.

Even though we've been hurt by the carelessness of others, the truth is we have hurt ourselves more deeply than anyone else ever could. We assume that other people fault us at the same level we fault ourselves—but believe me, they don't. We're more cruel to ourselves than anyone else could ever be. We can do to ourselves in ten seconds what no one could do to us in ten years!

When we tend to criticize ourselves, we'll assume that we're also **being** criticized. Instead of listening we are loved, we **listen we are judged**—and, of course, when we feel judged, we react by detaching from our partners, withdrawing our love, and judging them right back. It's a Herculean task to let ourselves be loved when we are in this mindset, and yet this is when we need it the most.

The fact is, you have been entrusted with a very important job—taking good care of yourself, and the best way you can do this is to stop beating yourself up. The person in the mirror needs your patience and forgiveness, not your constant criticism. Listen you are loved! When we listen we are loved, we can be returned to the grace of loving ourselves.

The rewards of listening we are loved

When Francine and I are sharing the leadership position at a meeting or workshop, one of the qualities people notice most is how well we work together. There is no competition or judgment. I empower her to lead the meeting and then I chime in whenever I think it's appropriate. Most of the time, Francine welcomes my interruptions, since they add special insights to the conversation. But sometimes, if she's in the middle of a thought and doesn't want any distractions, right there in front of everyone, she'll say, *"Hold on a minute, Lewie,"* and continue speaking. When that happens, since I trust her implicitly, I simply wait until my turn comes.

I remember a new Club member coming up to me after the meeting and saying in an astonished voice, *"I can't believe you didn't get upset by that! If my wife said 'Hold on a minute' in that way, I'd go ballistic."* I saw my old self in that moment, the part of me that was always looking for evidence to feel wronged or slighted. I realized that I trust Francine to always have my best interests at heart and to create the most value for the Club members—so I don't take it personally. When Francine speaks, I listen I am loved, and when I am in the presence of her love, I never feel slighted or diminished by her greatness.

However, if I am not listening I am loved, when Francine corrects me or makes a suggestion, I feel myself tighten up. There's a very ancient part of me that wants to blurt out: *"So, I'm not good enough for you, huh?"* But now I recover immediately from this reaction as I repeat my favorite mantra, *"She loves me, she loves me."* Then I can hear what she's really saying: *"I love you!"* instead of what I **think** she's saying (*"Lewie, you're an idiot!"*).

Years ago, if my youngest son Jonathan forgot to take out the garbage, it meant he had no respect for me. If my daughter Reppy left her cereal bowl in the sink, it meant she never thought of anyone but herself and couldn't possibly love me!

My life was spent listening to my inner conversation and believing my over-active imagination—I was a busy little bee and I got to be right—if I decided someone wasn't trustworthy, they didn't stand a chance with me. I faulted everyone for not measuring up to my standards. Now I know it's because I didn't trust they loved and valued me. I'm so glad that I gave this up. What a freedom I have now, and such a capacity to enjoy life as never before!

We all have the ability to do this. It's just a skill some of us haven't learned yet, and it takes practice. Like many other principles in this book, it's simple, but not easy. As we incorporate the new skills, part of learning this different way of being will be that we'll forget from time to time and go back to the old way. But the majesty of human beings is that we always have the ability to remember.

Trusting you are loved

Look around at the people in your life. Who do you really trust loves you? Your parents? Your partner? Your children? Your friends? **Trust** is defined as: *Firm reliance on the integrity, ability, or character of a person; to have or place reliance or confidence in, depend.*

How many of us live our lives knowing that we are absolutely, totally, unequivocally loved? Let's start with everyone's original relationship: our parents (you can answer this question whether they're alive or have passed on). My question is: **Do you trust that your parents love(d) you?**

I can hear many of you saying: *"Yes, yes, of course my parents love me."* But do you **really** know they love you? If so, then why don't you say *"Thank you for loving me"* when they tell you that you should manage your money better or exercise more?

Your parents have always loved you. When you were

an infant in your father's arms, he loved you with a fierce protectiveness that only a father can feel. When your mother held you and fed you, she felt a joy that had not yet been awakened within her. Beyond any of their fears and shortcomings, beyond whatever their issues were as human beings, your parents loved you with a love that was stronger than anything they had ever known.

I've met quite a few people who've said they know their mother and father didn't love them because they were given up for adoption. This concept even makes sense to some of us when we first think about it: how could anyone do that if they really loved their baby? However, rarely has anyone ever given up a baby because they didn't love him or her. In fact, often it's quite the opposite. This reminds me of a story about a man who served in the army in India during World War II.

Some American soldiers were leaving India, heading up the gangplank to board the ship that would carry them home. The dock was filled with women from the area, who rushed the ship, called out, and thrust their infants toward the GIs, crying, "Please take my child with you! Please take my baby!" This man's buddy said to him with contempt, "Can you believe these people? Look at these women, wanting to give their children away like they're some kind of trinket. What sort of people could do such a thing?"

The man replied, "You idiot! These children are dying of starvation and disease. Their mothers are making the ultimate sacrifice—they know if we take them, their children will live. Wanting to give them away? Of course they don't want to, but because they love them so much, they're willing to never see them again."

Your parents loved you—and they had the same problem of forgetting that they were loved by **their** parents! They didn't trust that **they** were loved, so how could they pass that legacy to us? How long are we going to hold onto the notion that we are not loved? How much longer are we going to live with the pain of that erroneous belief?

I remember another story of two young priests who were on a pilgrimage in Asia; they came to a river and encountered an old woman. *She said, "Please, kind sirs, I am too ill to cross the river. Won't you be kind enough to help me?" One of the young priests kneeled down, lifted the woman into his arms, and proceeded to carry her across the water. The other priest waded alongside him, agitated and upset, chattering worriedly in his ear: "You must stop this now! You know you're not supposed to touch a woman, you'll be exiled from the temple. I'll have to tell the High Priest what you have done. Your parents will be ashamed of you and throw you out—you'll have no family, no friends, no home. Put her down, please put her down!"*

*The young priest carried the woman across the river and placed her gently on the bank. The woman thanked him and went on her way. But for the next ten hours as the priests continued their walk, the second priest kept on talking about the terrible thing that had occurred. He went on and on and on: "I will have to tell the temple elders! Everyone will be ashamed of you. You will be exiled. Why didn't you just put her down?" Finally the young priest turned to his friend and stopped. He said, "Listen, my friend, all I did was carry that poor woman across the river. You've been carrying her for thirty miles. When are **you** going to put her down?"*

That's a good question! When are we going to stop carrying around the same old burden about how unfair life is? How much more time will be wasted believing we are not loved? When are we going to put that poor woman down and get on with our lives? The answer could be now. It starts with the words...

I am loved.

This experience is available to us all. We must recover our God-given ability to let ourselves be loved. Our purpose in life is creating partnership with others—but there can be no experience of partnership without trust, and trust begins by **trusting we are loved.**

I'm sorry for the suffering you've gone through because you didn't trust that you were loved. I know it's been painful. I'm sorry that you haven't been honest with people for fear of upsetting them. But when we don't communicate, we are just adding more weight to our theory that we're not loved, and we **create** the experience of **not being loved**. We're right—dead right—again. When we communicate, we **create** the experience of **trusting we are loved.**

Trusting we are loved happens moment by moment

In each moment—now—there is the opportunity to trust we are loved. But we can't just say, *"Okay, I'll trust that I'm loved for the rest of my life."* We won't. We'll forget, so we'll have to practice remembering.

When we forget we are loved, we feel accused, attacked, misunderstood, unappreciated. We worry that we might upset someone. Each time that happens, we can become aware of our automatic response and remind ourselves that no matter what is happening—**we are loved.** Each time we forget is another chance to remember!

And what makes us forget? Well, people don't act the way we want them to! We want to be loved—but we want to be loved **our way.** We become attached to our ideas about the way love should be, so our partner may have a difficult time living up to that standard. When we want love to look a certain way, we often find ourselves trying to manage and control our partner's actions or emotions, which can cause all kinds of friction and conflict.

But why would anyone want to control another human being's actions or emotions? Because they **themselves** feel out of control—they don't trust that **they** are loved! People don't need to orchestrate or micromanage others unless they are afraid—usually of abandonment or rejection. When we trust that we are loved, our partners won't need to conform to a rigid structure or specific set of rules—our trust frees them to express themselves authentically, from the heart.

This doesn't mean that we shouldn't ask for what we want or let our partners know if something upsets us—these are important factors in any healthy relationship. The difference is, when we're letting ourselves be loved, those communications spring forth from a well of faith, not mistrust. When we speak our needs or grievances from that place of love, our partners are more likely to be able to hear us and give us what we need.

Letting ourselves be loved means just that: **allowing another person to love us.** Our partners can't help doing things that annoy or hurt us—and we all have our pet peeves—that's part of being in relationship. The place to always come back to, however, is *"I am loved."* A good way to begin is by becoming aware of what triggers you to forget—start to recognize what words or situations rob you of the experience of feeling loved.

When we're not trusting we are loved, we're at the mercy of the other person, the situation, our own thoughts. We give them such power over us! As we hold onto the past or cultivate our current complaints, we hoard our pain like a squirrel putting away nuts for the winter. Stop looking for nuts already! Stop trying to get what you already have. The past has passed—it's over—you, on the other hand, are still here! Rejoice in this moment and your ability to remember that, no matter what the circumstances, **you are loved**.

Every practice in this book has as its foundation the experience of trusting we are loved. We start here, and build out into the world from that place. It is up to each of us to be willing to relinquish our hold on the assumption we are not loved and to open ourselves to the reality that **we are**. This infinite heritage of love has been with us from the moment we were created—reviving its truth in our hearts begins the moment we say we're ready.

There is no time like the present to start a new tradition in your life—in honor of yourself and those who love you the most. Please listen and let yourself be loved. You are, you always have been, and you always will be loved. Trust.

CHAPTER 2

Listening with Compassion

When we are heard, we are healed.

What is compassion?

How do I define compassion—the path that has saved and healed me?

**Compassion: A very deep appreciation
of another person's feelings and experience.**

Compassion is *not*: **Pity, sympathy, feeling sorry for, relating to, identifying with**. It's not commiserating and saying, *"Oh, yeah, I've been there. I know what that feels like!"* We can have compassion for anyone who is feeling anything at anytime—whether we have had that same experience or not.

When we are in the experience of having compassion for another human being, we listen without judgment, without analyzing, without trying to fix the situation or needing to change them. One truth I have discovered is that the most natural thing in the world is to **evaluate** what is being said to us—to fit it into our own way of looking at the world. Instead of just **hearing**, we **react** in various ways: by defending, explaining or justifying, or by feeling the need to offer opinions or advice.

We say, *"Oh, I don't agree." "How can you be so upset about such a little thing?" "That's not the way I feel about it." "Oh, c'mon, it's not that bad!"* Judgment and evaluations are a given—we don't have to dig for them. But compassion, ah, that's a rare bird. Compassion is a conscious choice we make. We have to **create** or **generate** compassion, and when we do, an amazing thing happens.

The person in front of us is safe. They no longer feel alone. They think: *"Someone understands, someone really cares, someone really knows who I am."* There are few experiences more empowering than to feel completely known by another human being. In the act of listening with compassion, a person can be returned to the truth about themselves: *"I am okay. What I feel is alright. There's nothing wrong with me! I am loved."*

Compassion makes us wise

How many of us worry about saying the "right thing" to a loved one, especially when they're upset? When we are in the embrace of compassion, we don't have to worry. An insightful clarity comes to us, and we speak easily, effortlessly, straight from our hearts. When we listen with compassion, we are always appropriate to the situation.

Another factor that makes compassion unique is that it is a **choice** to be of genuine service to another person. It takes awareness to think before we judge, and to be willing to admit that our judgments are not necessarily

the truth. There's a bit of wisdom originated by an Indian chief that many of us have heard—**Before you can judge another, you must first walk a mile in his moccasins**. Even though the saying may be familiar, how many of us truly take the time to understand how someone is experiencing something? We take a quick look at the moccasins, and in the blink of an eye, decide what size they are, how they were made, what their comfort level is like, and how long they're going to last!

When I think of the gift of compassion, I'm reminded of a story that illustrates what it's all about.

A man sits on a subway on a lazy Sunday afternoon in New York City. It's a sultry day, quite warm, and people are dozing. Others are reading or talking softly. Suddenly the train stops, the door opens, and in walks a man followed by three children. He sits down and stares into space. The three children, however, immediately start running up and down the aisles, yelling and screaming, hitting people, pulling at their newspapers, and generally creating bedlam. Everyone is horrified and sends dirty looks in the man's direction, hoping he'll do something. But the man just sits, seemingly oblivious to everything.

Now the first man is sitting there thinking, "My God, what is wrong with this guy? Why isn't he doing something about these little brats? It's the parent's responsibility to keep children in line—what the hell is the matter with him?" But the man still sits, doing nothing, as the children run amok and the people fume silently. Finally the first man has held his irritation in check long enough and he turns to the other man. As evenly and diplomatically as possible, he says, "Sir, don't you think you should do something about your children?"

The other man slowly looks up and shakes his head apologetically. "You're probably right," he says sadly. "I know I should do something. But you see, we've just left the hospital and . . . well, my wife, their mother, just died. I don't know what to do with them. And I guess they don't know what to do with themselves either." And the first man's heart broke—he wanted to reach out and embrace this anguished soul. All his anger and impatience vanished in the presence of his compassion for this human being who was in pain.

This story reminds me how common it is to judge other people when all we have is our interpretations. When someone cuts us off in traffic and speeds away at 90 miles an hour, do we usually think: *"Gosh, she's in a hurry. I wonder if she just got a call that her son was injured on the monkey bars at school and she's racing to be with him"?* Or do we think: *"What a jerk!"* (or worse!)? In every situation, we have the choice to see people and circumstances through compassionate eyes.

We can start looking for ways to do that now. Think of a person you are having difficulty with. Imagine how you would feel if you were that person, with their particular set of circumstances, personality traits and history. Now create a compassionate thought about him or her. Congratulations! You have just started on the path towards healing that relationship. The truth is, everyone is our teacher—it is no accident that certain people are in our lives. We have much to learn from the ones who frighten, anger, or otherwise upset us—we must honor their presence and strive to look for the opportunity our struggle with them may mask.

Compassion is not the same as comforting

I remember times in my life when I've been frightened and people tried to help me by telling me not to be afraid. In their well-meaning way, they tried to give me comfort. But the strange thing was, I didn't feel comforted—I became annoyed because I felt they dismissed my feelings.

Why do we try to comfort? The bottom line is because we love people so much we want to protect them from pain. However, there is another reason that will make it clear why sometimes we are quick to wipe away the tears: when someone is upset, **we** become uncomfortable.

Since many of us have been conditioned to think that upsets are bad, our first impulse may be to alleviate the pain—it's not easy to be in the presence of intense emotions. And if their upset has something to do with us, it's especially challenging! Feelings like anger, grief, disappointment, or fear in another person can stir up a myriad of unpleasant reactions, and we understandably want to do whatever we can to make it better, fast. We want to fix it—and if we're honest, it's as much for our sake as theirs. On the other hand, when we respond with compassion, we can simply **be** with another person without having to change anything.

When we try to comfort others, we often unwittingly deny their experience, telling them subtly that they shouldn't be feeling what they're feeling. When people think they're being discounted, they tend to close down and get even more upset. I'm sure you can remember a time when this happened to you. What did you really want? Assessments? Opinions? Analysis? Or did you just want to be heard, knowing that they profoundly honored and fully appreciated your experience?

Advice is often premature

Advice, feedback, thoughts, suggestions—all of these are valid and important contributions we make to one another. The tricky part is offering them when they can actually be utilized. Until our partners have been heard, odds are they won't be able to benefit from even our most astute observations.

It usually looks like this: our loved one presents a problem, and we, being caring, loving partners, immediately want to contribute feedback that we **know** would help (and we're probably right)—so we blurt it out before we've listened with compassion. Most likely, our partners reject our advice, accuse us of not hearing them, and blame us for upsetting them more! We then feel resentful—*"Fine, do it your way! Why'd you ask for my help if you don't want it!?"* Our partners are in worse shape than before, stuck with their original upset as well as the added pain of not being heard.

We need to ask our partners if they want our thoughts and ideas—simply put, we need to ask permission. Asking *"Do you just want to be heard?"* or *"Would you like some feedback?"* is a good way to find out what your partner wants.

Sometimes simply being heard is all a person needs in order to discover what's true for them or what action they want to take. Often, when I just listen to someone with my whole heart and don't speak at all, they'll suddenly say, *"Oh, I just realized what's really going on! I know what I need to do! Thank you so much!"* And I smile, because I haven't done anything, really. I just made it safe for them to be exactly the way they were, and in that loving environment, they found their own solutions. When we are heard by another, we discover our own truth.

All feelings are valid

It's easy to see the impact not being heard has on children. Consider the feelings of a little girl named Wendy, and I'm sure you'll remember experiencing similar emotions at some point in your life. Wendy looks upon her new baby brother for the very first time and understands instinctively that life as she knows it is about to change. Confused and frightened, she wails: *"I hate him! I hate him and I wish he never came here!"* Her parents, immediately alarmed, might say, *"Oh, Wendy, don't be silly—you don't hate your new baby brother! We know you really love him!"*

In that moment, Wendy hears: 1) **her feelings are bad**, and not only that, 2) **they don't even exist!** To Wendy's young heart, those messages are extremely hurtful. Her feelings would have been validated, and her tender spirit honored, if she had been told gently, *"Oh, sweetheart, we understand how you can feel that way. This is all so new and different, and you're afraid that because of the baby, we might not love you anymore. Come here, darling, we want to hold you."*

Here's a story of another child—Michael has just awakened from a terrible nightmare. He has dreamed of a hideous monster and, now wide awake, is sure that the creature is still in the room, waiting for him to let his guard down so it can strike. Michael screams for his parents and they come running, wanting to minimize his trauma as quickly as possible. So they say, *"Darling, it was only a bad dream; the monster isn't real—it's just your imagination. There's nothing to be afraid of—see, we'll show you."* They turn on the lights and everyone gives the room a thorough investigation: no unwanted lifeforms in the closet, under the bed, outside the door. The parents are satisfied. *"See, no monster! There's nothing to be afraid of."*

But Michael isn't so sure. To him, the monster **is real**, as alive and solid as any other object in the room. Of course, everyone knows that the monster Michael "saw" was only in his head, but every fiber of his being told him that there **was something to be afraid of**. It is an experience that cannot and should not be denied.

At one time or another, all of us have been in the position of both Michael and his parents. We've all been denied our experience, and we have denied others theirs. How much more loving to say, *"Oh, sweetie, I'm so sorry you're afraid. It must be so scary to feel that a monster is in your room. We'll stay right here beside you until you fall asleep."*

At the core, we are all children who have experienced not being listened to with compassion. We have wounds and scars from the times we shared our innermost feelings and they were dismissed or invalidated. As adults, when we experience being profoundly heard, when our feelings are honored as being natural and right **for us**, a miraculous healing takes place. We experience a long-overdue sense of peace and contentment.

Another story I love about a parent and child reminds us that the need to be listened to is at the heart of everyone:

> *While in a toy store, my husband and I overheard a mother and her small daughter discussing the dolls. "What does it do?" the child would ask about each one. The mother would answer, "It talks," or "It wets," or "It cries."*
>
> *The activity dolls were very expensive, so the mother tried to direct her little girl's interest toward an ordinary*

one that was more reasonably priced. "Does it do anything?" the child asked.

"Yes," the mother replied, "it listens."

The little girl eagerly reached for the doll.

Compassion is magic

Compassion is true magic—because when we listen this way, we can make things disappear. Things like anger, fear, loneliness, old hurts, long-standing resentments. When an emotion or experience is expressed and validated, it has a tendency to decrease in intensity or even vanish completely. When it is met with resistance or negative criticism, its natural reaction is to get stronger.

How does this work? Well, let's go back in time to when it all began—our childhood. Let's say we were four years old and wanted a certain cereal for breakfast. Mama said no, she didn't have any more, it was all used up. Would we like something else? We understood what Mama said, but we didn't want anything else. We wanted our cereal and we wanted it **right away**! Mama patiently explained that it had been eaten, why she couldn't get to the store until later that afternoon, that we could have it for breakfast tomorrow—all perfectly reasonable explanations.

But we were four years old, and we didn't care about any of that! All the reasons Mama gave didn't help—in fact, hearing them made us even more frustrated. In our little minds, the situation was very simple: We just wanted the cereal, and instead of giving it to us, Mama was telling us why we couldn't have it! Soon, Mama began to get exasperated at our ravings, until she finally said, *"Look, I don't want to hear anymore! You're driving me crazy! We don't have the cereal! Either have something else or go hungry!"*

Well, we didn't like that and probably didn't like Mama for a while either. Eventually we would have settled for another cereal or gone to our room hungry and sulked. But what if Mama had said, *"You really want that cereal, don't you? I wish you could have it—I know it's your favorite. Wouldn't it be wonderful if we had a magic wand, we could wave it and poof—there it would be, right in your bowl!"*

Imagine the instantaneous comfort of knowing our needs are important to Mama! We feel immediate relief: We still want the cereal, we still don't have the cereal, but we feel heard, known, and cared for. We may be disappointed, but our feelings have been mirrored back to us in such a way that we feel honored: *"Mama loves me—she also wishes I could have my favorite cereal."*

When we **recreate** (verbally reflect back) the experience of another person, a marvelous thing happens—the pain dissolves or lessens. When our communications are not met with resistance of any kind, we are able to let them go. This principle is not unique to our example—there is a scientific basis for this phenomenon: **two things cannot exist in the same space at the same time**. In other words, what happened between you and your Mama could be broken down into the following interchanges:

"I want the cereal."
"You can't have it."
"I want the cereal!"
"You can't have it!"
*"I **want** it!!!"*
*"You can't **have** it!"*
*"I don't care what you say! **I WANT IT NOW**!!!!!!"*

As you can see, this goes nowhere and creates lots of upset for both of you. But look what happens when Mama listens with compassion, validating and **recreating** your experience:

"I want the cereal."

"You want the cereal."

"Yeah, I want it now!"

"You want it now."

"I want it, Mama, I really do!"

"I know you really want it, you really, really do."

Before long, our plea has no place to go except the atmosphere. As long as Mama keeps being compassionate and simply acknowledges what we are feeling, our protests eventually run out of steam. Two things cannot exist in the same space at the same time. When we listen with compassion, we can liberate our loved ones from a lot of needless suffering.

Listening with reaction

Remember the last time someone didn't listen with the purpose of recreating your experience? Though not the type of response just described above, most likely, their remarks were an attempt to show their support: *"I can't believe he did that to you! I don't blame you for being mad—why, only last week the same thing happened to me, and I refused to put up with it! Don't let him think he's got the upper hand—he'll walk all over you!"* While this kind of commiserating might initially justify our feelings, it certainly doesn't solve the problem. In fact, it may make it worse, because having someone agree with us enables us to get mired down in self-righteousness—*"Yeah, I always thought he was an idiot, and now someone else thinks so too!"* This kind of listening tends to solidify our positions and prevents us from seeing the bigger picture.

Now remember a time when someone disagreed with or judged you—discounting your feelings as wrong. What if you said to your partner, *"Honey, I feel kind of lonely—I don't feel you've been paying enough attention to me."* And your partner yelled: *"How can you say I haven't been paying enough attention to you? Last week, not only did I work my full-time job, but I made dinner every night, did your laundry, cleaned the house, took care of the kids and paid all the bills while you were running around with your big important international business friends! What more do you want?"* How do you feel after a response like that? Less lonely? More loved?

But what if your partner responded this way: *"Oh, darling, I'm so sorry you feel like you're not getting enough attention from me—I can hear how hurt you are. I've been so busy with everything that I haven't realized how stressful things are for you right now with your job... it must be painful to be under so much pressure and then come home and not feel welcome."* Ah... can't you just feel the sigh of relief in your soul—the release of anxiety? Doesn't the pain just ebb away, perhaps even completely? How glorious to be listened to this way by those we love... how healing to be heard... how freeing to know that someone else can make our feelings as important as their own.

The diagram that follows demonstrates the different reactions and responses we may have, depending on the way we listen.

Behavior of Listener	Reaction of Speaker	Result
Offers sympathy or agreement	Feels upset is justified ("I'm right!")	Upset remains; grows stronger
Gives advice prematurely	Feels defensive, judged, dishonored	Upset remains; speaker withdraws
Argues or disagrees	Feels defensive, judged, and not heard	Upset remains; anger and resentment build
Listens with compassion	Feels heard and honored	Upset dissolves; experience of safety and partnership is created

Learning how to listen

For many of us, listening is not much more than **waiting**—waiting quietly for the other person to finish so we can have our turn. We may seem patient and attentive while they're talking, but inside we're having a lively conversation with ourselves, planning what we're going to say or trying to figure out what we think they want to hear.

Instead of just hearing what is being said, our brains are working overtime—judging, evaluating, reacting, disagreeing, wanting them to change, wanting to help. **Our attention is on *ourselves*, not the other person.** It's a pretty good bet that if suddenly your partner said they were furious with you, your first reaction would be to get defensive and perhaps feel falsely accused. You might even get angry at your partner—a normal reaction, to be sure. However, if you were listening with compassion, you would be focused on **them**—their discomfort—not yours. Simple, but not easy!

When we listen with compassion, our knee-jerk reaction to leap to conclusions and prepare our defense takes a back seat to our commitment to make it safe for our partners to express themselves.

When our partners say to us, *"I really need to talk to you, I'm upset,"* we frequently tense up, preparing for the usual barrage of complaints and readying our response. How can we truly be there for them when we are so concerned about **how we're doing**? Why is it so difficult to look over there at this person we love and hear their despair, frustration, anger, loneliness, confusion, or whatever else they're feeling?

What are we so afraid of? Being attacked and hurt? What are we protecting by not being open to what is being said to us? Perhaps we are not trusting we are loved, perhaps we think we won't be heard when our time comes—**if** it comes? Probably all of the above and more. But we have to gently remind ourselves that compassion must be **created**, and the process begins **with us**. As in so many aspects of relationship, someone has to take a stand and introduce this new way of listening. Someone has to make that crucial first move—don't wait for your partner to make it.

Looking over there

A qualitative shift happens when we take our attention **off ourselves** (*"What does this mean to **me**? How will this affect **me**?"*) and put it over there, on our partner (*"I know it's difficult for him to say these things to me—it's important that I make it safe for him to tell me what he's really feeling."*). Compassion is about relating to the **experience** of another human being—not necessarily the content— listening for how they are feeling, not just the specifics of what they are saying.

When we listen without compassion, we're not present to what's going on in the moment. We're listening to some other conversation from the past or an imaginary one that hasn't happened yet. We need to train ourselves to rise above one of our most habitual, human responses: **to add meaning to what is being said to us**. It starts with the willingness to relinquish our need to rob, in any way, our partner of the experience of being heard.

How to listen to others *without* compassion

- **Keep the focus on yourself.**
- **Wait to hear what they'll say and how it affects you.**
- **Look them in the eye, but pay close attention to your own thoughts and reactions.**
- **Jump to conclusions whenever possible—you know what they're going to say, you've heard it all before.**

- Interrupt every time you see an opening or when you disagree.
- Worry about what you're going to have to do about what they say.
- Decide how you want them to be different.
- Judge and evaluate what's wrong with them, and get annoyed that they're stuck in the same old patterns.
- Don't let your guard down just in case they're blaming you.
- Decide how you're going to defend yourself against their accusations.
- Give them advice whether they asked for it or not.
- Figure out the answers to their problems—after all, why would they be talking if they didn't want your help?
- Enlighten them as to what's wrong with their point of view—don't forget to give them your infinite wisdom.
- Change the subject.
- Make them feel guilty for having their feelings.
- Comfort them and try to make them feel better, or tell them it couldn't possibly be as bad as all that.

Unfortunately, this list represents the way most of us have listened and been listened to. Many of our interactions have had some of these components. I know it can be uncomfortable to realize how we have all listened in the past, but please don't be too hard on yourself or your loved ones—remember, we've all done the best we could. However, let's explore what we have to look forward to!

How to listen to others with compassion

- Keep the complete focus on the other person.
- Let your partner talk at first without interrupting. If they hesitate, ask encouraging questions such as: *"Is there anything else?" "Is there more?"* If your attention wanders to your own thoughts, move it back to them as soon as you notice it.
- Be genuinely interested—find out what they're thinking and feeling.
- If it's appropriate, ask questions which will help you more fully understand what's going on with them.
- Imagine what it would be like to *be* them, having their emotions and experiences.
- Remember, even if they're complaining about you, they're always speaking about their own pain.
- Notice if you feel the need to judge, defend, justify, explain, or criticize, and let these reactions go. Put your attention back on your loved one. You'll have a chance to communicate. Be patient.

- Validate or recreate (reflect back) their feelings and statements when appropriate.

- Notice if you have a desire to give advice, offer help, make suggestions, but don't do it yet. There will be time for all of that later. Right now, your job is to *listen.*

- Listen the way you want them to listen to you.

- Remember that you are loved, and welcome their communication as a gift and an opportunity for healing. If they're upset with you, remember the mantras... *"She loves me... she loves me..."* or *"He loves me... he loves me...."*

If this list seems daunting, overwhelming, or too good to be true, that's understandable. Whenever we attempt to break free of well-worn patterns, the new ways may seem unattainable at first. The truth is, it will take time to learn these new skills and incorporate them into your life, but you will be pleasantly surprised at how quickly they can become a part of you.

The healing power of compassion

Listening with compassion is a healing experience for the one who listens as well as the one being heard. We manifest our higher selves when we have compassion for another person. When we lay aside our judgments and critiques, we find ourselves in the presence of our own generosity and goodness.

Most of us could make long lists of the things we don't like about ourselves—but how many of us can speak about our innate greatness without feeling like frauds? The truth is, we all need to be reminded of our good qualities. We've been told to be brave and confront our shortcomings and weaknesses head on, but how many of us have been supported in getting back in touch with how worthy we are?

Compassion takes away the need to judge ourselves: *"I shouldn't be feeling this way, there's something wrong with me, I'm making a mountain out of a molehill, why can't I just stop being upset?"* When someone listens to us with compassion, they give us an opportunity to mend our relationship with ourselves. It opens a door through which we can accept our humanity with love: *"The way I'm feeling is okay, there's nothing wrong with me, I am fine just the way I am."*

Compassion as a means to self-acceptance

Most of us have believed the notion that we must already have mastered a concept or skill in order to contribute it to another person. For instance, we've thought that we can't support another in breaking through a fear unless **we've already done so**. I believe the opposite is often the truth—and that is indeed welcome news. Sometimes we can learn our most valuable lessons by helping others learn theirs. In the act of serving another person, we are served exponentially. When we give someone else that which we want for ourselves, we increase our ability to receive it.

Since we are usually harder on ourselves than we are on others, it can often be easier to have compassion for another person. In the act of creating compassion for someone else, we become aware that we deserve it too. We give other people much more leeway—we're much more open to forgiving someone else or seeing their positive side.   We can actually jump-start our ability to have compassion for ourselves by having compassion for others.

Creating compassion is a function of intention and will: if you can't do it for yourself, do it for another. Once we begin to develop our capacity to generate compassion, it will spring forth from us effortlessly. Most of us think we need to "have it all together" to be there for one another—the truth is, all we need to have is the **willingness to be there.**

How can having compassion for others help us with our quest for self-acceptance? Because we'll see ourselves in them. We'll see our own fears and self-criticism reflected in the eyes of another. We'll see our heart in the heart of the other, and in having compassion for their humanity, discover it in ourselves. The most exciting part of this is that we can learn to love ourselves through our love of another. It is a gift that returns to us a hundred-fold. We are here to create partnership—to practice love and forgiveness, and that includes loving and forgiving **ourselves**. Compassion for another is a place to begin.

On the other side of the coin, when we find ourselves in a situation where it is difficult for us to have compassion for another, we can tap into the experience of having compassion for ourselves to see our way through. Remember—**we are all one heart**. We are all deserving of our own and one another's compassion.

Listening to our partners

Listening with compassion to our partners has its own set of unique challenges. This person that we live with and love so much has the ability to drive us crazier than anyone else in the world! Most of us have, if we've been with our partners for any length of time, a whole storehouse of grudges, resentments, and unspoken disappointments. When they speak, we often hear their words through a thick gauze woven of all the times they didn't listen to **us**; we can have a hard time accessing compassion because of these unfulfilled promises and shattered dreams. And if our partners are upset with us, we often feel attacked and want to defend ourselves, which makes it extremely difficult to listen with compassion.

Conflict is part and parcel of everyone's life, but most of us have not been taught how to listen with compassion! So we've done the best we could, and have reacted and responded to our partners' words and upsets the only way we knew how—thinking they were criticizing us, adding negative meaning to what they said. The less our partners felt heard, the less they could hear us.

Why can it be so hard to hear our partners?

Ironically, it's often the very people we most need to hear us who listen to us the least. Why is it so hard to listen with compassion to our life partners? Why do their requests, comments, and upsets cut us to the quick when the same words from someone else roll off our backs? Because we take it **personally**—we are emotionally involved—and we have a hard time hearing what they're saying without thinking it is somehow a criticism of us. We don't listen that we're loved—we listen that **we're judged**.

Of course, this isn't hard to fathom when we realize that often our partners are, indeed, blaming us for their troubles! And since human beings tend to listen from a place of being accused and misunderstood, it's easy to see why we have so much difficulty being in the presence of what our partner is saying to us, without attaching our own interpretation to it.

However, when we add undue significance to what is being said, we are again having too much **attention on ourselves**. As we train ourselves to listen with compassion, we become able to put aside everything but our willingness to **hear** our partner's communication as a declaration of their experience, not a condemnation of us.

When our partner speaks to us, no matter what they are saying, first and foremost, they need our compassion. He or she is not the enemy—only a human being who needs, above all, to be heard by us. Simple, but not easy.

Everything else that needs to be communicated to resolve the issue can be done inside the embrace of compassion. **The mistake most of us make is trying to work on the specifics of the situation before we have heard one another—that's what causes us to fight**. Listening with compassion is at the foundation of all communication—when it is present, the natural outcome is always an end to suffering and a return to truth.

Deflection

Instead of listening, one of the most common things we do is to **deflect**. Deflection means: *To turn aside or* *cause to turn aside; bend or deviate*. We deflect by turning aside what is being said and shifting the focus **off ourselves**. Then we're off the hook—we don't have to be accountable for the subject matter of the communication. Deflection is something we do when we are afraid, when we feel the need to protect ourselves from danger—it's a universal survival technique.

Deflection can be subtle—it's hardly ever as obvious as in the following exchange:

> *"Honey, I've been making an extra effort to listen to you with compassion more and I don't feel like you've noticed."*

> *"Hey, that reminds me—I don't feel appreciated for some of the things I've been doing."*

Deflection in its most potent form usually follows this pattern: what if you'd been worrying all day about an argument that happened at breakfast, and you—in the interests of communicating and moving on—said something like this:

> *"Honey, I'm still really upset about what happened this morning—I feel so bad about the things we said and I still feel hurt and angry. Can we talk about it?"*

and instead of hearing you, your partner responded with:

> *"Why do you always bring these kinds of things up as soon as I get home from work? You know I need to wind down—you're so inconsiderate. All you think about is yourself!"*

or

"You're so emotional! Why can't you just let go and forget about it? Why do you need to keep rehashing the same old stuff over and over?"

or

"You're always blaming me for everything! I know you think it's all my fault—well, I'm not about to get on that merry-go-round with you again. No way!"

It's easy to see how the focus changes—**it's no longer about your upset** or your attempt to reach out—suddenly, you're on the defensive, trying to justify your feelings or explain why you brought the whole thing up in the first place. Instead of addressing your needs, you're having to deal with the annoyed deflection of your partner, and guess what? The actual issue at hand doesn't get resolved! Sound familiar? Of course—we've all done it.

Men and women often do this without even being aware of it—and end up infuriating one another. *"Why can't he just **hear** me?"* *"Why does she always have to twist things around so that it's **my** fault?"* Well, it's simple—instead of listening we are loved, we listen we are **accused**, so everything that's said becomes more evidence that we've done something wrong. We're so busy defending ourselves or denying the deed—it's almost impossible for us to get our focus off our own thoughts and have compassion for each other.

Advice can look like criticism

Another frequent conflict arises in the area of advice. We may think: *"Why else would she tell me about her situation at work if she doesn't want my help?"* After all, why would anyone bother telling someone about a problem they're having unless they're looking for a solution?

Giving advice prematurely can result in a situation that's terribly frustrating for both people—for instance, let's say Bob offers Jane advice, and then he can't believe it when she gets even more upset—at **him**! Since all Jane wants is to be heard, when Bob starts in with his good ideas, she feels once again that her feelings don't matter to him—and she's insulted that **he** thinks **she** can't fight her own battles! Now, the odds are that Bob doesn't think that at all—he may be just trying to be supportive and show he cares—but to Jane it feels like he's not really listening.

In this situation, both people are being called forth to have compassion for one another: Bob needs to just hear Jane and honor her ability to come to the truth for herself, only giving advice when appropriate, and Jane needs to remember that Bob loves her and that one of the ways he expresses it is to offer help. As in all dynamics with couples, there are lessons to be learned for both people. **We may think our greatest power is in our speaking, but in fact, it is in our listening**. There is no substitute for being heard!

Here is a letter from a woman to a man—but it could have been written by any of us:

> *"When I ask you to listen to me and you start giving me advice, you haven't done what I asked. When I ask you to listen to me and you begin to tell me why I shouldn't feel that way, you are trampling on my feelings. When I ask you to listen to me, and you feel you have to do something to solve my problem, you have failed me, strange as that may seem. Listen.*

*All I asked you to do was listen. Not talk or do. Just hear me. I can **do** for myself—I'm not helpless. Maybe discouraged and faltering, but certainly not helpless. When you do something for me that I can and need to do for myself, you haven't helped me. But when you accept a simple fact that I do feel what I feel, no matter how irrational, then I can quit trying to convince you and get on with the business of understanding what's behind that irrational feeling. And when that's clear, the answers are really obvious. And I don't need advice.*

Irrational feelings make sense when we understand what's behind them. Perhaps that's why prayer works, sometimes for some people, because God is mute and he doesn't give advice or try to fix things. He just listens and lets you work it out for yourself. So, please listen and just hear me. And if you want to talk, just wait a minute for your turn. And I promise, I'll listen to you."

Compassion in daily life

Each day we are given countless opportunities to listen with compassion. Sometimes we have infinite patience and can hear anything from anyone, other times we may be stressed or upset and don't have a lot to give. When we are having difficulty listening with compassion, we can still honor our partners by telling the truth:

- *"I'm having trouble listening to you with compassion right now. I'm sorry."*
- *"I want to have compassion for you but I'm feeling really defensive and it's difficult to not take what you're saying personally."*

- *"I know I should have compassion for you but I can't."*

Instead of sitting there stewing in judgment or anger while our partner speaks to us, statements like these are helpful because telling the truth about where we are gives us room to move on. A Club member shared a question she once asked her husband: *"Honey, I'm really hurt and it's hard for me to have compassion for you right now. Can you have compassion for that?"* Her husband told the group that her question made it possible for him to look over at her, get his attention off himself, and it worked!

Let's look at some situations where compassion turns these upsets into opportunities for healing. Notice what happens with this couple. It's the end of the day and they've just gotten home from their jobs. She arrived a few minutes earlier, and as he comes through the door, she says:

She: *"Hi, honey. How was your day?"*

He: *"Actually, it was lousy. I was just about to sell the new client on our marketing strategy, and now I'm afraid we're going to lose the account altogether. I felt really good about my ideas, and my boss told me a few weeks ago that it looked really good, but the client wasn't wild about it at all. I mean, if I lose this account, I think I might as well kiss that promotion good-bye. I'm really upset.... I don't know what to do."*

She: *"Well, I did suggest that you let other people get involved and not insist on doing it your way all the time."*

He: *"What? What do you mean? You know I've put everything I had into this deal!"*

She: *"I knew this would happen! I've told you over and over—don't take everything on by yourself, but you never listen! When are you going to pay attention to what I say instead of thinking I've got air between my ears?"*

He: *"That's a hell of a response—typical! I come home dead tired and scared to death and all I get from you is siding with the enemy. It'd be nice if there were one place in the world where I felt appreciated!"*

She: *"Oh, great! Now we're into self-pity. You've got some nerve—don't you talk to me about not being appreciated! I not only have to work all day, I also do all the shopping, cooking, laundry, and cleaning! And **you** don't feel appreciated. Give me a break!"*

He: *"I've had it—I can't take any more of this crap. Get away from me—I can take care of myself. I don't need **anything** from you!"*

How upsetting for both of them. But why couldn't she have compassion for him? After all, he wasn't upset with her when he first began speaking. Well, to begin with, when he told her he might not get the promotion, she got scared. She couldn't hear his fears because she was **focusing on her own fears**—and at that moment, her ability to have compassion was impaired.

Everything he said also touched another one of her sore spots: *".... he never pays attention to what I say, he thinks I'm stupid; if only he'd listened to me, he wouldn't be in this mess; I don't feel appreciated, and he wants me to appreciate him? Fat chance!"* She couldn't have compassion for him because her own fears and resentments got in the way. Let's look at what could happen differently in this same situation.

She: *"Hi, honey. How was your day?*

He: *"Actually, it was lousy. I was just about to sell the new client on our marketing strategy, and now I'm afraid we're going to lose the account altogether. I felt really good about my ideas, and my boss told me a few weeks ago that it looked really good, but the client wasn't wild about it at all. I mean, if I lose* this account, I think I might as well kiss that promotion good-bye. I'm really upset.... I don't know what to do."

She: "Oh, sweetheart, I'm sorry. What an incredible disappointment, especially after all the work you've done."

He: "Thanks. It's been a really rough day."

She: "I can imagine—this has been such a long haul and you've given it everything you've got. Do you think they'll give you another chance?"

He: "I don't know—I sure hope so. I'm scared because this could be the second account I would have lost this year. I talked to Al about it and he said we could get together about it tomorrow, but I feel bad having to go to him."

She: "I know you do—but I'm proud of you for asking for help. That took a lot of courage. Besides, it means that I've been right all along when I've tried to support you to not do it all by yourself—and you know how much I love to be right!"

He: "Do I ever! (laughs) But thanks—I appreciate your saying that. And you **were** right! You know, I'm also upset about maybe having to let go of some of the plans we've made, thinking that I was going to get promoted. I mean, I still might, but I can imagine you must be concerned—I know you really wanted to take that trip."

She: "Yes, I really do, and I hope we still can. I must admit I do feel anxious about it—when you said you might lose the account, I got scared too."

He: "That's understandable. We've both been really counting on it. Why don't we make dinner together and talk about it some more? And thanks for listening, and for loving me so much. You're the greatest!"

What an experience, to be listened to like this! Such a relief—it's like drinking the sweetest, coolest water when we are hot and thirsty. When compassion is bestowed upon us, suddenly our own compassion is available in abundance. On the other hand, when we judge, criticize, or attack, it's no surprise that we often get back the same from our partner.

With our couple's second try, we know that they'll be able to handle whatever challenges come at them, because they are in partnership. In their first attempt, there was no hope of working out their difficulties because they were adversaries. Without compassion, our partners can look like mortal enemies, and we all know how agonizing that is.

Here's another couple—this time it's the man's opportunity to create compassion. This conversation happens over dinner in their favorite restaurant—their first real time alone in weeks. However, things don't go quite as well as expected:

He: *"I've been really looking forward to this, honey. It's been so long since we've gone out."*

She: *"Oh, so have I. I've been wanting a chance to talk to you without any distractions. Can I just jump right in?"*

He: *"Sure. What's going on?"*

She: *"Well, I've been avoiding bringing this up, but I've really been miserable lately. I feel so alone and worthless, especially now that things are going so well for you at work. I feel like I'm drifting... like I don't have a purpose anymore."*

He: *"Hm. Maybe it's time you went back to work— it'd keep you busy and get your mind off things."*

She: *"What do you mean by that?"*

He: *"Well, like I said, I think the problem is you don't have enough to do. It's obvious that you have too much time on your hands—that's why you're so miserable."*

She: *"Really? Well, I don't think that's the problem at all—I think **you're** the problem!"*

He: *"What?"*

She: *"The more successful you get, the more distant you become. I can't remember the last time you really listened to me as if you cared. You're so self-absorbed and stressed out that it's becoming impossible to live with you."*

He: *"What the hell are you talking about? I think I'm a bloody saint. I work all day and come home to you every night no matter how much I'd rather go out for a drink with the guys! Why do you always blame me for your unhappiness?"*

She: *"Oh, all of a sudden this is about how **you're** getting shortchanged—no surprise there! You are so selfish! All you do is think about yourself and your precious little corner of the world. You're the reason I'm so miserable! I can't believe I was so excited about planning this date. Let's get out of here—I've lost my appetite!"*

It's so obvious how much they are hurting. If only he'd listened with compassion! Let's give our friends another chance:

He: *"I've been really looking forward to this, honey. It's been so long since we've gone out."*

She: *"Oh, so have I. I've been wanting a chance to talk to you without any distractions. Can I just jump right in?"*

He: *"Sure. What's going on?"*

She: *"Well, I've been avoiding bringing this up, but I've really been miserable lately. I feel so alone and worthless, especially now that things are going so well for you at work. I feel like I'm drifting... like I don't have a purpose anymore."*

He: *"God, honey, I'm really sorry to hear that. It sounds so painful."*

She: *"Thanks. I've been scared to tell you... afraid you'd think... well...*

He: *"Darling, I'm so sorry you've been scared to talk to me about this. Please trust that I love you. I really want to know how you feel—please tell me."*

She: *"Well, I seem to have lost confidence in myself and I'm afraid that you'll... well... lose interest in me. I know it sounds stupid, but I feel insecure and abandoned. Sometimes you get so wrapped up in what you're doing, you seem to forget all about me. Lately you seem more concerned about your work than you do about our relationship. If you remember correctly, I'm the one who made sure we got out tonight—I feel if I left it up to you, we'd be home in front of the TV again! I know I should have told you this before, but I've been afraid to bring it up... afraid you'd get upset with me."*

He: *"Oh, sweetie, I'm so sorry. I never wanted this to happen. I know I've been busy and preoccupied, but I didn't realize the effect it was having on you—I hadn't realized you felt so strongly. I never wanted to hurt you or leave you behind—you're the most important thing in my life. You're the reason I've been able to get as far as I have. I've been really thoughtless—please forgive me. And I'm so glad you told me. I love you so much!"*

She: *"I love you too. Thank you so much for listening. I'm so glad we're talking this out. Now, let's eat!"*

This conversation may sound too perfect to be real, but I promise that you can learn to have this type of compassionate interaction with one another—and each time you do, your partnership will grow stronger.

Having compassion can be challenging

It's much easier to have compassion for someone when they are upset about something that doesn't relate to us. The real task is to have compassion for people who are:

- **Accusing, judging, or blaming us**
- **Confronting us in a dominating, intimidating manner**

- **Convinced that we are wrong and it's all our fault**
- **Not being honest about how they really feel**
- **Withdrawing or taking themselves (or their love) away**
- **Rejecting or intentionally trying to hurt us**

If we examine the list above, we can easily see that all the items actually point to the same experience: when our partners are hurt or afraid, they may feel the need to hurt or frighten us. Because we are human beings, we usually react viscerally against the attack, trying to defend and/or launching a counterattack. We need to look over there and realize that this person in front of us is in pain.

They're suffering—why else would they be trying to wound us? They're attacking or withdrawing—so they must be feeling the need to protect themselves! This is when compassion, in its highest form, can save us. Our goal is to trust that this wonderful person in pain loves us—no matter what they say or do, they love us. If we can listen without lashing out at them in blind retaliation or wanting to hurt them, we will have come far in our journey towards partnership.

To have compassion means we must be willing to look beyond our reflexive reaction to what our partners may really be saying, what they really want. The amazing thing is that compassion immediately casts out fear.

<blockquote>

We cannot be afraid of someone for whom we have compassion.

</blockquote>

The people we know who are intimidating need the most compassion from us. We may or may never be able to find out exactly what shaped their lives, but when we are able, even for a moment, to see how afraid, how **human**, another person is—we no longer fear them.

Compassion as a way of life

Being listened to with compassion doesn't mean that we now have *carte blanche* to willfully and carelessly dump all over our partner and then fault him or her for not hearing us (although sometimes we might do this)! We all need practice in learning how to speak so we can be heard and how to ask for what we need more effectively. In creating partnership, we must have compassion for what our partner has experienced from our being extremely upset and perhaps inappropriate. **The more attention we pay to our partner's well-being, the more we'll find ourselves communicating in a way that can be heard.**

As we listen with compassion to those around us, we are giving them one of God's greatest gifts—the gift of being truly known by another human being. In this glorious experience, we are safe, we are without fear, we are one heart. When we are heard, we are healed. Compassion is the place to begin.

Listening with compassion, like trusting we are loved, is not something we master and never forget. We need to practice and practice and practice—all the while having compassion for ourself and our partner as we learn.

When we listen with compassion, we truly honor the person in front of us—listening with our hearts, not our heads. We can begin right away—with ourselves, with the next person we see. In the space compassion creates, issues are resolved, balance is restored, love is rekindled. Compassion is an angel, watching over us as we discover our way through the forest—empowering and illuminating each step we take.

CHAPTER 3

Apology

Apology is not an admission of guilt,
it is an act of love.

The phenomenon of apology

Let's say that you are in an argument with your partner, slinging mud everywhere, feeling out of control, and wishing something would happen to stop the insanity. What if your partner suddenly said:

> *"Honey, wait. I want to apologize to you. Everything I've been saying in this argument has been a defensive reaction to that comment you made earlier. I didn't listen I was loved, I made up a lot of things without checking with you to see if they were true, and I've been judging you ever since. I apologize for not hearing you and for saying all those careless, thoughtless things, and for the pain I've caused. I know I've hurt you deeply. I'm so sorry, and I love you very much."*

Wouldn't that be a miracle? And wouldn't it completely change the course of the conversation? You just couldn't continue to fight! Not only would you probably be able to create compassion for your partner, but you'd most likely become aware of your part in the upset, and apologize too. At the very least, you'd be speechless with delight! Apology has the power to rescue us from a deadly undertow **immediately.**

Apology can instantly defuse even the most intense anger. It can make us sane and put us back on the road to recovery. Apology can transform both the current condition and our distant past. Even when we feel completely wronged, a sincere apology is a cool cloth on a fevered brow. Apology changes the climate of our relationships from a battle of right/wrong to a meeting of heart and soul. As we work towards partnership, practicing the art of apology is one of our most valuable tools.

Of course, the benefits of apology are proportionate to the high cost of not apologizing. Sometimes human beings make mistakes—significant mistakes that do real harm. Where there is no apology, there can often be no closure. For instance, I remember a news item a couple of years ago that was a poignant example of this.

A man who had been convicted of murder and imprisoned for seventeen years was suddenly exonerated and set free. After years of investigation, detectives had finally tracked down and brought in a confession from the real killer. It was quite a coup for the police and restored everyone's faith in the law. However, it was a dark day for the justice system. Obviously the jury had made a grievous error.

So now we have this innocent man who has spent and sacrificed **seventeen** years of his life behind bars—can you imagine the suffering he must have endured, doing that much time in prison for a crime he didn't commit? The story explained how his name had been cleared and described the joy of his friends and family. But when the man was interviewed and the reporters asked him how he felt about being a free man, he didn't even address the question. He only said, *"No one apologized to me. All I wanted was for them to say 'I'm sorry, we were wrong,' but no one said* **anything***. They just gave me my watch and my wallet and that was it. I've lost seventeen years of my life, and no one even apologized."*

He didn't talk about how relieved he was to be getting out or about his excitement for having another chance at life. It was unbelievable to him—no one even said, *"I'm sorry."* So tragic, yes, and yet so human. These people who put him behind bars just didn't have the courage to admit they'd made a huge, life-altering mistake. Just think of the good they could have done this man if they had apologized—in that moment, his healing process would have begun. Instead, he was left with yet another injustice and more resentment. What a missed opportunity! If we could only live our lives in the presence of how much of a difference we can make when we apologize.

Many of us have hoped we might get by without cleaning up the messes we've made, and sometimes it looks like we will. After all, if we don't talk about it, then the nagging discomfort will just go away by itself, right? We all know the truth by the pain we've experienced when we've been hurt by others who never admitted their mistakes or apologized. An undelivered apology can fester inside a human heart for decades, diminishing our ability to be present to the majesty of our lives.

What is apology?

Apology simply is: *An acknowledgment expressing regret and compassion.*

Acknowledgment means to admit the existence, reality, or truth of. If we acknowledge something, it means that we're stating that it is so. There is no evaluation in acknowledgment. It is merely a statement of fact.

In learning to apologize, we are **not** being called on to pass judgment on what happened. **We are simply being asked to *acknowledge* that something we did or didn't do affected another person.** That's all—our job is to make a statement of fact about our partner's feelings, not explain or justify. Just as we discovered in having compassion, declaring that another's feelings exist is supremely important. When we apologize without any other qualification, we are in essence stating that our partner's experience is real and valid.

When we offer an apology, we're also not saying we're bad or wrong. Apology is appropriate to give whether we did something on purpose, or didn't really mean to do it. Most of the time we don't set out to hurt our partners. We're not on the warpath looking for ways to damage people. But we are human—we cannot help making choices that may affect others.

Often excuses, stories, justifications, explanations, and reasons masquerade as genuine apology. We may offer an abundance of these and more, yet our partner might still insist that we haven't apologized! We say, *"I'm sorry, but—."* We qualify our apology, diluting its effectiveness. Then we become frustrated and say, *"I said I was sorry, didn't I!? I've apologized for this ten times! What do you want from me?"* We may even wonder why our partner doesn't feel honored or taken care of!

So we apologize—why? Because it's the loving thing to do, and it works! It takes guts to stand up and say, *"Yes, I did that, and I apologize."* It takes integrity to put aside our need to be right, to be accountable for our actions. Whether or not we are at fault is no longer the relevant point of discussion. The real essence of the conversation is: *"How can I get back into partnership with the person I love? How can I take care of this person who is in pain?"* Apologize!

An apology is a compassionate statement that says we are willing to take responsibility for the consequences of our actions and to make someone else's feelings more important than our desire to be right.

We learn to apologize when needed, for significant and (seemingly) insignificant things. *"I apologize for forgetting to turn off the oven and burning our dinner."* In a pure apology, we don't go into a song and dance about **why** we forgot, even if it's a truly fascinating reason. Our only purpose is to take responsibility for what we did without excuses—expressing the unvarnished truth about how we affected another human being. Simple, but not easy!

Apology creates affinity

The first step is being willing to **acknowledge** what happened, whether or not we feel we had anything to do with it. If our partner gets upset during a conversation, we obviously had something to do with it, even if all we did was mention the word "taxes" and then our partner became worried because the papers the accountant asked for are still missing. In this instance, we clearly didn't set out to upset them, but in fact, he or she **is upset**. What's important now is to apologize—not for having done anything wrong, but simply to show respect and compassion for our partner's feelings.

"Honey, I'm sorry you're upset about the taxes. I know you've been concerned about that all week."

When we apologize like this, we are not trying to fix or change anything, we are just expressing compassion. We are acknowledging the existence of our partner's experience and validating it. Discussing how you're going to find the tax documents comes later, and it'll be a lot easier since your apology will have created a harmonious environment. When we receive an apology, we feel honored and appreciated. Apology creates affinity because we immediately experience being known—our well-being is important to our partner.

It's never too late to apologize

A good friend of ours is an emergency physician. Recently he was attending a convention in which doctors and administrators had come together to hear from people who had experienced problems with emergency care. There were three cases presented.

A woman told a heartbreaking tale. One day she received a phone call from an emergency room informing her that her son had been injured in a motorcycle accident. (In truth, he had already died, but the person calling didn't tell her!) She frantically raced to the hospital, uncertain of his condition, and when she arrived the staff told her she wouldn't be able to see him—no explanation or comfort was offered. Traumatized with worry and fear, she pleaded with the hospital personnel to at least give her some information, but hours went by and no one told her anything. She asked over and over again to see her son, but they would not let her go to him.

Eventually they told this poor woman that her son had, in fact, died. She became hysterical and demanded to see his body. When she was again told that she could not, she began screaming: *"I must see him, for God's sake—he's my son! I need to say goodbye, I need to be with him! Don't you understand? He needs me now more than ever!"* Unfortunately she was never allowed to go to her child and say her farewells.

As soon as the woman finished speaking, one doctor after another stood up to explain to her why this had happened. She was given excuses and justifications based on hospital policy and protocol. The doctors felt it necessary to defend the hospital staff and give reasons to minimize the damage that had been done. And as you can guess, the woman became, understandably, very upset.

Finally our friend stood up and said, *"First of all, I want to apologize for what happened to you. Please accept my apology for all the pain and suffering you went through, and for your untimely loss. I'm so very, very sorry.*

Secondly, I want to thank you for the contribution you've made to me today. You see, I have never been trained how to take proper care of the families who love the people who are injured or who have died. Your story has made me aware of how important it is to communicate fully, and include the family in what's going on. Thank you so much for showing me what I need to do to become a better doctor."

When I heard this story, I was so proud of our friend. Here he was, apologizing for something that he was not even a part of—apologizing on behalf of others who weren't able to do it! What a bounty of gifts he gave everyone that day—not only to this grief-stricken mother who finally heard what was long overdue, but to all the health care professionals who were present. The healing power of apology is obvious when we see the restorative effect it can have. When we apologize, even our deepest wounds can finally begin to mend.

How I've learned to apologize

In the process of teaching myself how to apologize, I've discovered some simple phrases that speak directly from and to the heart. I invite you to adopt these phrases and incorporate them into your life—or similar words that feel natural to you and your partner.

"I'm sorry you're upset."

This is a statement to use when your partner is distressed, especially if it's clear that it has nothing to do with you. Just this simple apology communicates your concern—*"I'm sorry you're upset."* It's simply a compassionate observation, but it says so much: that you notice and care about them. It can be used as a loving gesture in countless situations.

"I'm sorry you're upset, and if I had anything to do with it, I apologize."

When you suspect you may have contributed to your loved one's upset, these words are very welcome. You may not even be aware of what you've done (or what they think you've done), but you're pretty sure they're upset **with you**. This statement shows that you are conscious of their pain and that you are willing to be responsible for your part in it. (It also works particularly well if you are feeling **unjustly** accused—when they are blaming you and you **know** you didn't do anything.)

When we acknowledge our partner's upset and the possibility that we contributed to it, we represent ourselves as an ally.

"I'm sorry I upset you and I apologize."

In this case, you are certain that you had something to do with their upset, even if you may not know exactly what it is. Your job is to get back into partnership so you can address the issue. These words show your partner that he or she means more to you than justifying or defending your position. When we state our accountability right away, we set the tone for the entire interaction.

I remember the day one of these statements first came to me. Francine and I had set aside an afternoon to make love. As we were doing some last-minute clean up from lunch, we found ourselves in the middle of an argument. Within moments, we were totally estranged—she was upset in the kitchen and I was upset in the bedroom. We were hurting so badly. No matter how I turned it over and over in my mind, I couldn't let go of the anger and resentment. Suddenly I had a thought.

I went into the kitchen and said, *"Francine, I'm so sorry about what happened but I can't let go of my upset. Can you help me? I'm sure right now you don't care what I feel, but I really need your help."* And she said, *"You're right, I don't give a damn how you feel!"* I kept pleading with her that it would help me if she would say the following words: *"Lewie, I'm sorry you're upset, and if I had anything to do with it, I apologize."*

Eventually she agreed and asked me to repeat the words for her: *"Lewie, I'm sorry you're upset, and if I had anything to do with it, I apologize"*—I had to say them five or six times. When she finally said the phrase, the most incredible thing happened—all my anger, disappointment, and resentment completely disappeared! It was a turning point. I had been waiting to hear and speak those words all my life! I knew then we had found an entrance into a whole new world. For myself, whose upsets have historically been quite intense, learning to apologize has done more than help me...it's saved my relationships and made me sane.

I've even learned to apologize to myself when I'm upset. I know that may sound a little silly, but when we realize how many negative things we say to ourselves in the course of a day, it doesn't seem all that strange.

For instance, if I start to have critical thoughts about myself, I say:

"Lewie, I'm sorry you forgot you were loved."

If someone is unkind to me, I would say:

"Lewie, I'm sorry you were hurt. I'm sorry you're upset."

This kind of reassuring self-talk really works for me. When I am alone, I've learned to tell myself the things I would want to hear from a loving parent or a kind friend. We've all been listening to our inner voices all these years anyway, so why not have them be compassionate ones? Apology in any form is an act of kindness.

Why do we have difficulty with apology?

For many of us, our first encounter with apology was as punishment, meted out by others: *"Apologize to your sister!"* or *"How **dare** you say that to me! I demand an apology!"* When we were children, apology was something we avoided—after all, having to apologize meant we were **wrong**! And since apologizing meant admitting we were wrong, why be foolish enough do it?

Far from a redemption, an apology was an expression of failure or weakness. We'd shuffle up to our sister, shamed into owning up to whatever crime we'd perpetrated—a crime we often felt unjustly accused of. We'd think, *"She started it first. The only reason I tore her painting was because she called me stupid! **She's** the one who should apologize."*

Mumbling, *"Sorry,"* under our breath, our voice barely concealing our resentment, we might have heard Mama or Papa correct us: *"Don't use that tone of voice! Say it like you mean it!"* But how could we mean it? How could we feel true remorse or take responsibility for what we had done when we felt like it wasn't our fault? It wasn't fair. Having to apologize just dug us deeper into the pit of shame. Humiliated, we'd slink back to our room with instructions to *"feel sorry about what you've done."* Apology was nothing more than a punishment—it did not look like a very good thing under any circumstances.

When we get to the heart of why it can be difficult to apologize, it makes sense when we realize how strongly we associate it with guilt. And what is guilt, really? Is it the act of being responsible for something we did? No—guilt is a poor disguise for responsibility. In guilt, there is tremendous self-reproach—we are **bad**. We haven't just **done something** bad, **we are bad**. So if apology is an admission of guilt, by apologizing we are in effect saying: *"I'm bad, I've done something bad, I should (and do) feel bad about it, and you are entitled to harbor bad feelings about me."*

However, when we separate guilt from apology, we realize that they are actually diametrically opposed.

Feeling bad about something is a way that many of us have **avoided taking responsibility**. After all, if we feel bad about it, then we're off the hook, right? Think back to a time you received an apology that was laden with guilt and shame. It probably didn't have any positive effect on the situation—most likely, it just compounded the problem.

We can't be present to our partner's needs when we are weighted down by self-reproach. **Feeling bad keeps the attention on ourselves**. We must strive to understand this distinction between guilt and apology, become accountable for our actions, and make being in partnership more important than "feeling bad."

We must keep reminding ourselves that apology is an act of love. It is designed to bring us closer together. Being accountable for our actions doesn't mean we have to approach our partners with our tails between our legs. Feeling remorseful about what we've done is not a prerequisite for apology. We just need to do it.

Apology helps us embrace our humanity

Our resistance to apology is understandable because it relates directly to how hard we are on ourselves. The truth is, we are human, and yes, we can be insensitive and occasionally even cruel to our loved ones. We are not evil people, but we can harm one another. For many of us, it's virtually impossible to admit we've made a mistake— that something we did damaged another. We give ourselves so little permission to just be a person doing the best we can—we think we need to be flawless. And since we're spending so much time trying to live our lives perfectly, being accountable for what we did or didn't do is not an easy task.

Yet the irony is that to be truly human is to embrace all our strengths, weaknesses, greatness, smallness—to love and forgive ourselves. Doctors "practice" medicine—why can't we let ourselves "practice" being human?

When we are no longer rigidly protecting the illusion of perfection, we can let down our guard and demonstrate the character to own up to whatever we are responsible for, without invalidating our basic worth.

In the avoidance of our flaws being found out, it's natural to want to defend ourselves or put the blame on another. Yet, as we continue to trust that we are loved, it becomes apparent that we are big enough to apologize when we've hurt another, separating our accountability from having done anything **wrong. We are not wrong**! Through apology, we can reclaim our innate goodness and lay down the shameful, leaden anchor of guilt.

The fine art of apology

I've discovered that the more I can direct my apology to the heart of the matter, designing it to fit the specific need, the more power it has. As we practice apology, we will find that giving an overview of exactly what occurred can be very beneficial to our partner. In the examples that follow, the apology creates an opening for further communication—a doorway to conversation and resolution—and leaves our partner feeling honored and valued.

- *"I'm sorry I'm late. I should have called when I realized I wasn't going to be able to finish on time—I know how you worry about me getting into a car accident when I'm tired. I apologize for not being considerate and for anything I did that upset or frightened you."*

- *"Darling, I want to apologize for the way I've been acting lately. I've been so anxious about the situation at work that I've been snapping at you for days. I've been blaming you for things that aren't your fault and being really critical of you—two things that I know upset you a lot. I want you to know that you're not doing anything wrong—I'm just really stressed right now, and I'm so sorry for taking it out on you."*

- *"You know, honey, I've been thinking about last night and some of the things I said at the dinner party. I remember at least twice I disagreed with you and judged you pretty harshly in front of your friends—I know you hate it when I do that, and I can understand why. No wonder you were so quiet on the way home. I'm so sorry."*

When we're not in partnership, it affects everything—our foundation is rickety. When we build a bridge of love through apology, we rise above our need to justify, explain, excuse, or minimize the effect we have on our partners. Each time we transcend pride by putting our partner first, we strengthen our integrity and enrich our souls. Learning how to apologize appropriately is vital to the health of our relationships.

After a lifetime of avoiding apology, it now lives in me—so much so that sometimes people don't understand why I'm apologizing. I remember a meeting where I was talking with a group of children about what frightened them. They began telling me stories about times they were scared. I found myself saying, *"I'm so sorry you were afraid. How terrifying to feel so alone. I'm so sorry that you didn't feel loved and taken care of."*

Wide-eyed, one of the boys said, *"Why should you apologize? You didn't do anything!"* And I said, *"Yes, that's true, but I'm just sorry you were afraid—I'm sorry you were in pain."* The children looked at one another, pleased and surprised at how good it felt to hear those compassionate words from an adult. How healing it is to tell someone that you know how it is for them, that you feel sorry about what they went through! How we honor each other with our apologies!

Apology is an invaluable tool—it can be used to address a current issue, to repair old wounds, or to be given as a gift to represent someone else in the recipient's life. I have apologized to people on behalf of their deceased mothers or fathers, and they have sobbed with joy at finally hearing the words they longed for as a child.

All we ever wanted was an apology—we could have forgiven almost anything if we'd just heard, *"I'm sorry."* When someone takes responsibility for what they did and how it affected you, isn't it much easier to forgive? And when someone keeps deflecting the blame and making excuses, isn't it virtually impossible? We've spent a lot of time being wounded by the absence of apologies toward us as well as our inability to give it to others.

Sometimes it seems that apology is so missing from our world that I feel like apologizing for everything and everybody—*"I'm sorry for the way I am. I'm sorry for the way the world is. I'm sorry that life is not fair. I'm sorry that people can be cruel. I'm sorry that sometimes I wish you were different. I'm sorry that I can be judgmental and self-righteous. I'm sorry that I can't promise you I will never say anything to hurt you ever again. I apologize for anything I have ever done that has disappointed you, frightened you, dishonored you, or robbed you of your peace of mind. I apologize!"*

The heroism of apology

Apology is an act of bravery. We apologize because we are courageous beings. We are strong enough to admit not only our unintentional deeds, but also the acts we committed in retaliation that may have hurt another human being. We apologize because in doing so we lay down the weapons of war and make being in **relationship**, not being **right**, our highest priority. We apologize because it is simply what we do to create partnership.

Apology offers many rewards, the richest one being a renewed sense of feeling profoundly respected by our partners—an experience we all deserve. When we take full responsibility for our actions, without blame or guilt, we treat ourselves and our partners with dignity.

> **Apology is not an admission of failure and weakness—it is an act of courage.**

As we begin to trust that we are loved and to listen with compassion, practicing apology is our next skill to master. It may be challenging at first, but it will get easier. After awhile you will do it spontaneously and effortlessly, and wonder how you ever lived without it!

When we realize that giving an apology does nothing but enhance our relationships, we will offer it freely. When we find it doesn't diminish or weaken but in fact strengthens us, we will be grateful for every opportunity to express it. The more we trust that we are loved, the more generous our heart becomes, and the easier it is to take care of our dearest ones. Apology sustains our partnerships and leads us onward toward forgiveness.

CHAPTER 4

Forgiveness

Forgiveness is a gift
we give ourselves.

The power of forgiveness

Forgiveness is the cornerstone of partnership. To **forgive** means: ***To renounce anger or resentment against***. Without forgiveness, we cannot move forward in life. We are stuck in the past, unable to be in the present moment. Forgiveness, or the lack of it, is at the core of our greatest miracles and most profound tragedies.

Shakespeare's Romeo and Juliet lost their lives because their families, the Montagues and the Capulets, would not forgive one another—they could not even remember what they were fighting about, but that did not matter. All that mattered was they were at war, and this war cost them dearly.

The story of Romeo and Juliet still compels and moves us even now because of what happens at the end. After all the bloodshed and hatred, the two great houses realize at last how much their feud has cost them, and they finally stop fighting—at last setting their differences aside as they bury their beloved children.

They extend the hand of friendship and vow to honor each others' children after death, their grief uniting them in compassion. The price for this transformation was indeed high, but forgiveness was the ultimate reward. Romeo and Juliet's legacy was peace between their families. Without this ending, Shakespeare's tale would have been unbearably sad and have no lasting value—why continue to tell it, in so many ways and for so many years, if the lesson is not one of healing?

"To err is human, to forgive, divine." These words of eighteenth-century writer Alexander Pope say it all. We are human and sometimes hurt one another. The hurts can range from minor day-to-day annoyances or disappointments to significant breaches of trust—broken promises or acts of betrayal. In any lifetime, there will be things we do and say that will hurt the ones we love. We **will** err—it is part of being human. But we also must be able to redeem ourselves—we all deserve a chance to make amends.

That's where the divine part comes in. In forgiveness, we express God's grace—we are, by forgiving, in essence granting complete absolution and redemption. We relinquish our right to punish, cling to resentments, hold grudges. We give ourselves and each other permission to move on, free of baggage and history, able to progress without the burdens of the past. Forgiveness fosters our well-being when we know that no matter what happens, we will forgive and be forgiven. In an environment of love and forgiveness, we thrive.

That's what happens in an ideal world, but in most relationships, it's not that easy. We say we forgive, we may even think we do, but some part of us holds onto a little piece of pain—keeping it hidden like a dagger in a strongbox. We think we've forgiven our partners, but the next time they hurt us, we may find ourselves opening the box, taking out the dagger, and using it against them. We may have on the surface forgotten the injustice done to us, but on a deeper level, we haven't really forgiven.

When we are living with another human being, we are given countless opportunities to forgive—our partners can "push our buttons" like no one else. It may not seem significant, but each time we choose not to forgive, we drive a wedge between us and our loved ones. It's as if each resentment is a sheet of plastic wrap—every one seemingly crystal clear and incredibly thin. But stack enough of them up on top of one another and the stack becomes cloudier and thicker, until it's completely opaque and impossible to see through.

It may take awhile for the resentments to build up between ourselves and our partners, but when they do, they become an impenetrable wall that keeps us from perceiving one another clearly. What we see instead are all the unresolved issues—the shadows of the past have eclipsed our ability to be with one another in the present.

When that happens, it can feel as if we don't love each other anymore. If something isn't done to rectify the situation, the relationship may eventually die. However, miraculous things occur when people begin peeling back the layers and tearing down the walls. I've seen this countless times with couples who make a conscious, committed choice to save their marriages—as soon as they begin communicating, apologizing, and forgiving, the experience of love returns as if by magic. They can't believe it—they're in love all over again. The truth is, the love never went away—it was just buried.

Forgiveness is not condoning

Like apology, forgiveness comes to us with a few misconceptions in tow. For instance, many of us feel that forgiving our partners is tantamount to saying what happened was okay—that by forgiving, we are excusing their behavior and granting them license to do it again.

If a young child gets angry and tries to get back at his mother by breaking a lamp, Mama doesn't say, *"Oh, that's okay, honey, Mama understands. It's okay to break lamps when you're upset. I forgive you."* But she can help the child make an important distinction when she says, *"I am furious at what you **did**. It is **not** okay to break lamps when you are angry. But I love you, and I forgive you. Now I'm going to hug you until you calm down, and then we'll talk about other ways you can express your anger."*

Perhaps a loved one has done something that we deem "unforgivable"—a betrayal or careless act that causes a seemingly irreparable rift in the relationship. It is during these times that forgiveness can bring us back from the brink of disaster. Great harm has been done, to be sure, but if both people want very much to mend the break and to rebuild the partnership, it can be done—and forgiveness is the key. **We do not excuse or condone the act by forgiving**. The damage is real, and the trust must be earned again over time. However, true forgiveness is necessary if we are to recover from these difficult moments. The healing may take some time, but forgiveness is the first step.

Compassion is at the heart of forgiveness

Our old and faithful friend, compassion, has its hand in all of this. If we are able to find the way through to compassion—to have a very deep appreciation for our partner's feelings, motives, and experience—we can forgive on a much more profound level than we ever thought possible. Compassion lights our way toward forgiveness.

The mother with the angry child was able to separate what occurred from who did it. While not approving of the deed, she had compassion for **why it may have been done**. A loving parent understands that children who are in distress may act out inappropriately, and will look for the underlying cause. When we can look at what has been done through the eyes of compassion, we see far more than what we see through the eyes of condemnation.

Think of something that your partner has done, either recently or in the past, that you feel you can't or won't forgive. Now imagine it from the place of trusting you are loved and having compassion. Why do we feel justified holding onto our need to punish our partners? What has us resist letting go of the hurt? We have our reasons:

- *"I can't forgive him—he hurt me too much."*
- *"If I forgive her, then she'll take advantage of me again."*
- *"I'll forgive him when he's been punished enough."*

- *"He'll think I'm weak if I forgive him, and he'll lose respect for me."*
- *"Forgiveness is for saints—I just can't let go of the resentment."*

It takes a lot of energy to hold onto resentment. But what do we have to give up in order to forgive? First and foremost, we need to let go of whatever payoff we are getting by holding a grudge or continuing to punish—and that usually means **giving up the need to be right about being wronged**. When I forgive, my heart is stronger than my ego. It is only the ego that needs to be right—the heart just wants to love.

One of the most effective ways to punish another is to withhold affection—to take ourselves away. We feel justified in doing this since we feel we have been mistreated. But who do we really punish?

A Club member told me a story about her relationship with her husband. He had a habit that upset her greatly—whenever he'd get intensely involved with work, he'd stop paying attention to her, almost completely. During the first year of their marriage her pattern of reaction was the same: she'd get angry (quietly), withhold her love (silently), and hope he would notice and start being romantic again. When he didn't "get the hint," she'd get angrier, and even more sullen and hostile, hoping fervently that he'd figure out she was unhappy and change his behavior.

She became critical of him, impatient, made cutting remarks and answered his questions with grunts and dirty looks, feeling she had no choice other than to act this way. Finally he would finish whatever project he was on, and the minute he did, she'd go back to being kind, and he'd become attentive again.

After doing this three or four times over the course of that year, she began realizing that during those episodes she was in tremendous pain. The truth was that she loved her husband and wanted to be affectionate, but she was so hurt that she felt compelled to protect herself. She discovered that in her punishment of him, she was, in reality, punishing herself even more. It was so painful to hold her love back, so draining to keep up the hostile attitude and coldness.

In that moment of awareness, she decided to forgive him and instead trust that she was loved. In the instant she forgave him she felt lighter and more clear-headed than she had in a long while.

She immediately went to her husband and said, *"Honey, I've been withholding my love from you, hoping you'd sit up and take notice—but all it does is cause me pain. So I want you to know I'm not going to do that anymore. I forgive you and I know that you love me."* And do you know what her husband said? *"Oh, I'm so glad you said something! I know it upsets you when I get caught up in my work, but when you act so mad and distant, I get scared of approaching you and I turn to my work even more. Thank you so much for letting me know!"*

In this space of forgiveness, they talked about how they could better take care of one another during those times. She stopped punishing him and he gained valuable insight into his obsessive workaholic tendencies. He made a commitment to organize his schedule to include her, and in doing so, created a healthier, more balanced life for himself.

This couple has been married for fifteen years. Through this experience, they uncovered a treasure trove of information—most importantly, that the lack of forgiveness hurts us as much as it does our partner. When we do not forgive, we are shackled forever to the wrongs we seek to right. When we forgive, we set ourselves free.

Apology and forgiveness

Apology paves the road to forgiveness. It makes sense that once we apologize, forgiveness should be the natural outcome, and it frequently is. Why? Because, as we've all noticed in our lives, it's a lot easier to forgive people who are accountable for what they've done.

When George Washington chopped down his father's cherry tree, he took full responsibility—made no excuses, did not justify or explain. His father promptly forgave him, respecting him for his courage to tell the truth. Do you think this story would have become a permanent part of our proud American heritage if George had said the following instead?

"Well, yeah, Pop, I did chop down the cherry tree, but I didn't do it on **purpose***. I mean… I was just swinging the axe to get the feel of it and it sorta kind of slipped and hit the trunk real hard a few times… but, y'know, Dad, the truth is, if you look at the big picture, we really need the wood anyway, and besides, you've always said that I should do more useful things around the house…."*

George's song and dance would have stopped right there as Mr. Washington yanked him by the collar off to the woodshed for a whipping. Far from forgiving him for his reckless act and subsequent lie, George's father would most likely have punished him severely and mistrusted him in the future.

When someone we love freely admits to the part they played in whatever drama is unfolding, we find forgiveness so much easier. *"You're right, I wasn't listening to you, I apologize—I know that upsets you."* *"Yes, I did forget to mail the credit-card payment, I'm sorry. I'll do it right now."* *"It's true, I have been taking my frustrations out on you and the kids—I apologize for the pain I've caused you."* Doesn't it feel right to say thank you—and forgive?

But what about the other times—the times when people aren't able to be accountable for what they've done? How can we forgive them? Must we?

The answer lies within each of us. Only **we** can decide if we are ready to lay down our swords and have enough compassion to forgive. When someone hasn't been able to apologize or a loved one has died, we may then have to look to our own hearts to provide us with reason enough to grant them pardon. We must remind ourselves of the high cost we pay by holding onto our hurts. We must remember that it is **we** who benefit from relinquishing our need to exact vengeance, or to justify how badly treated we were. Please, put down the burden of resentment. Bless whoever has wronged you as they follow their path, and honor them and yourself with the unselfish act of forgiveness.

Forgiveness as a way of life

One of the most important lessons I've learned is that forgiveness isn't something I **do**, it's something I **am**. It all started when I began looking at the lack of forgiveness in my own life. I judged myself harshly and constantly—never let myself get away with anything—how could I expect to give anyone else a break?

It was when I met Francine that I realized how little forgiveness I had for my own and others' humanity. When I began having compassion, apologizing and forgiving her, I suddenly became aware that the person I really needed to forgive was Lewie. If I could forgive Francine and others in my life for making mistakes, why couldn't I forgive myself?

One day I noticed I was upset—I had forgotten that Francine loved me and had gotten angry at some reaction she'd had to a comment I'd made. Soon the usual litany of self-critical thoughts floated around in my head again: *"Now why did you go and do that? Can't you control yourself for a second? What's wrong with you?"* Suddenly I heard another voice, and it said, *"Lewie, I forgive you."* I found myself saying those words out loud: *"Lewie, I forgive you. I forgive you!"* Just hearing them had a dramatic effect—all the anger and judgment evaporated as I simply forgave myself for being me, for being human.

What a liberation! In that moment, I saw that although we are looking for forgiveness outside of us, in order to be sane **we** must forgive **ourselves** every day, all the time, sometimes hundreds of times a day if necessary. I began at that moment to see forgiveness as a way of life—**a context in which whatever I did or was done to me would be forgiven as a matter of course**. The pain of judging myself or others became too great—forgiveness was the only way through. *"I forgive you, I forgive you, I forgive you...."* —that became another one of my mantras.

I also discovered the true majesty was in **speaking** the words, *"I forgive you."* There is something about saying it, **even if you don't quite believe it in that moment**. Say it anyway—because **it is in the act of speaking that we can *create* forgiveness**. There is magic in those words! We may think them, they may be present in our hearts, but unless they are spoken, they have no power. Give yourself this opportunity to go beyond the fear of letting go of whatever you think you can't forgive—say the words to your loved ones.

To judge or resent takes no real effort, but forgiveness takes willingness. We become conscious of what we are holding onto for dear life, and we choose to give it up when we realize it is for the glory of truly being alive that we must forgive and be forgiven.

Tonight, when you see your partner, pick out one thing that has been bothering you, or some grudge you have been cultivating. Choose to forgive—just to practice. Speak the words *"I forgive you"* and see what happens. We've all been taught that the "three magic words" are *"I love you."* Those are wonderful words, but equally as important—in truth, sometimes even more so—is the powerful phrase, *"I forgive you."*

The gift of forgiving others

We can start by forgiving ourselves or by forgiving others. I believe God gave us other people to forgive so we could have the gift of forgiving ourselves. It is a sacred circle—**when we forget others love us, we are also forgetting to love ourselves**. When we have compassion for others, we remember that we deserve it too, and when we forgive another who has trespassed against us, the gift of forgiveness returns to us.

What a gift we receive from others when we have the opportunity to forgive them! I have discovered that the best thing I can do for my own health and well-being is to be in a constant state of forgiveness—I believe this is the key to healing all relationships in our own lives and in the wider world. I'm also sure it has been a big factor in my ability to heal from illnesses and stress and to enjoy vibrant health in my later years.

Forgiving our parents

Oscar Wilde said: *"Children begin by loving their parents; as they grow older they judge them; sometimes they forgive them."* We can see the striving of us all in this observation—we all start from love, go through judgment, and hopefully discover forgiveness. I am a very lucky man—my children have forgiven me, and this is an honor I do not take lightly. To be forgiven by my children has been one of the greatest joys of my life.

I would like all children to forgive their parents, **for their own sake**. Remember, in forgiveness we do not excuse or condone; we have compassion and we surrender our need to inflict punishment. It is such a godsend to forgive, and to forgive our parents is so vital. That relationship is the benchmark, the foundation for all the other relationships in our lives.

It is in the context of that relationship that we forged ourselves and made some of the most primal decisions about who we were. Some of those decisions were accurate, some not. Many of us have felt imprisoned by how we were shaped in our early years. **In our forgiveness of our parents, we unlock the gate to our self-erected prison cells and realize we have, and have always had, permission to be who we are: our own person.**

Our mother and father love(d) us so much—if only we could trust that love. I have spoken about this to hundreds of men and women in the Clubs over the years, and seen the weight lifted off their hearts when they forgive their parents. For our own sanity, whether or not our parents are alive or can hear us, we must forgive them.

For our well-being and serenity, I invite all of us to forgive everyone who has hurt or wronged us in any way. I ask this because to carry around these age-old resentments and anger takes such a toll—it makes it much more difficult to be here with the people who love us.

I remember one woman shared in a Club meeting how she hated her mother for yelling at her father and "driving him crazy." She didn't know what to do and couldn't understand how her mother could treat such a loving man so badly. Her father would complain to the daughter, so she had sided with him against her mother. I said to her, *"Do you think your mother was like that when she first got married? Your father has a part in this, too—she probably feels like there's no other way for her to be heard in this marriage. She may 'drive him crazy,' but men drive women crazy too, and I guarantee you this situation is not solely your mother's fault. I want you to have compassion for your mother, apologize and forgive her, and become friends with her."*

This young woman then went to see her mother. She apologized to her mother for the judgments she had and shared her feelings for the very first time. She then learned a great deal as she listened to her mother's side of the story, and gained a new, more balanced perspective about her parents' relationship. A caring closeness and trust began to develop. She forgave both parents, and in her forgiveness of them, opened the door for them to forgive each other.

Whatever our parents did, they loved us. If they could have been more aware and taken better care of us, they would have. Underneath all of their humanity, their flaws and mistakes, our parents love(d) us profoundly. Our partner loves us that way too—and he or she also deserves to live in an atmosphere of perpetual compassion and forgiveness. To live in that experience is to know peace.

The grace of forgiveness

I am very fortunate in my marriage, because Francine forgives me all the time. When I get frightened or forget I am loved, I take it out on Francine, the way we all do with our loved ones. I accuse her, blame her, judge her, I apologize, she forgives me. I live in the safety and presence of her constant forgiveness, and that keeps me going every day. I could not exist without it.

For the past two years, I have been battling and winning my war against cancer. Although I am completely cured and getting stronger every day, the process took a considerable toll on me and everyone who loves me. It was the most frightening experience I have ever had—my fear and subsequent anger was sometimes overwhelming, and it was only through the compassion and forgiveness of Francine and my family and friends that I made it through to be here today, ready to continue my work in the world.

During this process, I've learned much about forgiving others—it was a significant challenge to continually forgive those around me who could not understand or appreciate what I was going through. I learned what forgiveness is on a deeper level than I had ever thought possible: when one's life is threatened, it brings out both the best and worst in us, and it is through forgiveness that we are delivered. I am clear that in this case, forgiveness saved my life.

I remember sitting next to an elderly woman in the waiting room of my doctor's office one day and listening to a conversation between her and a younger woman—perhaps her daughter. The older woman asked, *"Is the doctor going to take an X-ray?"* and her companion said, *"I don't know—I guess we'll have to see if he thinks you need one."* About thirty seconds later she asked, *"Is the doctor going to take an X-ray?"* and the other woman said, without a trace of annoyance in her voice, *"I don't know—I guess we'll have to see if he thinks you need one."*

The older woman asked the very same question five times in a row, and the younger one answered the same way every time—patiently, kindly, lovingly. I was so moved to see this relationship in which the younger person had so much compassion for the older woman, forgiving her for forgetting and just answering the question again and again. It's not easy to do that. I was inspired and heartened to see the generosity of spirit and forgiving nature of this fine human being.

How many times has someone repeated something—perhaps forgetting they already told us—and our reaction is a curt *"I know—you told me already!"* We are so easily frustrated with our own and others' simple lack of perfection—let's try to be more tolerant and listen we are loved. Say *"Thank you"* when she reminds you of your dentist's appointment. If you say something and he doesn't hear or misunderstands you, say it again without impatience. A friend read me something lovely once: **Be kinder than you think is necessary**. We always have the choice to be kind.

God has given us limitless opportunities to practice forgiveness—of ourselves and others. From long-standing injustices and grudges to the day-to-day irritations and conflicts, forgiveness opens us, frees us, and brings us back to our hearts. **When we forgive, we are the beneficiary**—that is why we can forgive those who are no longer in our lives and still experience the relief of letting go.

When we ongoingly forgive our partners and loved ones, we give them the chance to develop and mature, unhampered by guilt or shame. In the act of forgiveness, we express our divine nature and wipe the slate clean, ready to create anew. Forgiveness is the child of the heart—nurture its loving spirit and limitless promise.

Decide to Forgive

Decide to forgive
For resentment is negative
Resentment is poisonous
Resentment diminishes
and devours the self.
Be the first to forgive,
To smile and to take the first step,
And you will see happiness bloom
On the face of your human brother or sister.
Be always the first
Do not wait for others to forgive
For by forgiving
You become the master of fate
The fashioner of life
The doer of miracles.
To forgive is the highest,
most beautiful form of love.
In return you will receive
untold peace and happiness.

—Robert Müller
Former Assistant Secretary-General
of the United Nations

CHAPTER 5

Speaking from Your Heart

*When we speak from the heart,
we always tell the truth.*

Why don't we say what we mean?

When children are hungry, they'll say, *"I'm hungry."* When adults are hungry, we turn to the person we're with and say, *"Are **you** hungry?"*

It almost reads like a joke, doesn't it, but isn't it the truth? Most of the time we don't say what we really want to say. Why? Well, at the heart of it, this is because we don't trust that we are loved. We also don't think we deserve to get what we want, or we're afraid we'll be misunderstood, or we're afraid of upsetting someone. So we learn to be great diplomats—subtly altering how we speak so that we don't endanger ourselves by telling the unvarnished truth.

When we want to get off the phone but we don't want the other person to think badly of us, we might say, *"Well, I'd better let you go."*

When we don't want to have sex because we're angry at our partner and we want to avoid a confrontation, we might say, *"I'm too tired."*

When we forget someone's name at a party, we might avoid them until we can ask someone else who they are— God forbid they should find out that we don't remember where we know them from. We often don't trust that we won't be judged or misinterpreted, so we've become masters at pleasing people or being covert. We don't want to appear pushy or dominating, so we sacrifice saying what we mean or what we want.

I remember one day I turned to Francine as we were driving around town and said, *"I'm hungry. I want to eat."* What a breakthrough! It felt fantastic just to say it like that!

We start by getting in touch with what we want, what we think, what we feel. In our willingness to be genuine and open, we'll make it easier for our partner to do the same.

For instance, if our partner asks us, *"Do you want to go for a walk?"* instead of saying yes or no, we might turn it back on them to make the choice. We may know exactly what we want to do, but we find ourselves saying, *"I don't know, what do you want?"* or we say yes when we want to say no—trying to keep them happy at our own expense. We're afraid they might be disappointed, or feel rejected, or be annoyed with us. It seems like a smart idea to just keep the status quo even though it goes against our preference.

But every time we do that, we cost ourself and our partner a small piece of our energy and aliveness. Every time we say yes when we want to say no, we are not trusting we are loved, and we create mischief. You know what I mean! Do they want us to walk with them if we don't **really** want to? Do we need to say yes just because they asked, to get their approval or make sure they're not mad at us? What a drama we invent about what they want! All he or she said was: *"Do you want to go for a walk?"* The rest of the script we write ourselves!

Many of us are often afraid to be honest. We've all learned how to manage the fear of being authentically who we are. But try this on for size: Let's say your partner asks you if you want to go for a walk, and you don't care to at that time. Try something outrageous for a change: **Answer the question**! Don't embellish it or explain. Just say, *"No, thanks."* We're so afraid of their reaction, we think we need to go through a whole production instead of just giving a straight answer.

This reminds me of another piece of wisdom I have tried to live my life by—**"Answer questions and acknowledge statements."** What I mean by that is to distinguish between the two and give the appropriate response. Simple, but not easy!

How often do we do that? We often answer a question with a question, or a statement with an answer that it doesn't warrant. For instance, here's a couple of examples of not answering a question and the mischief that ensues:

• **He:** *"I have this thought that you're feeling upset, are you?"*

She: *"Why should I be upset? You're the one who's always upset."*

He: *"Well, you don't have to bite my head off!"*

- **She:** *"Do you want to go to a movie with the Sterns?"*

  He: *"Why do we always have to go to the movies with another couple? Why can't we just go by ourselves for once?"*

  She: *"What's wrong with going out with friends? You're such a stick-in-the-mud!"*

Obviously, there's more going on than meets the eye in the two interchanges—these couples have some communicating to do. The point is that when we don't simply answer the question by speaking from our hearts, we impair our ability to deal with what's going on. Here's how both situations might have played out differently:

- **He:** *"I have this thought that you're upset, are you?"*

  She: *"Well, now that you mention it, yes, I am."*

  He: *"I thought so. I'm sorry. Do you want to talk about it?"*

- **She:** *"Do you want to go out to the movies with the Sterns?"*

  He: *"No, I don't. I'd rather go out just the two of us."*

  She: *"Really?"*

  He: *"Yes, and the truth is, I think we go out with other people too much. I want more time alone with you."*

  She: *"I didn't know you felt that way. Thanks for telling me!"*

We often feel the need to editorialize our answers. For example, someone may ask us, *"Do you want to go get an ice cream cone?"* We might be tempted to say, *"Wow, that would be nice, but I really shouldn't. I'm trying to cut down on dairy products right now. But you go ahead, don't worry about me."* What we really want to say is: *"No, thank you."* We don't have to be other than the way we are, and we don't have to explain why!

When we don't speak from the heart, it doesn't do anybody any good. If you're at your partner's office party and want to go home, don't sit in resentful silence for hours, not telling the truth because you think they'll get upset. Instead of hoping they'll notice how miserable you are and get the hint—tell them what you want! We don't need to waste precious time trying to figure out what our partner's response is going to be. When we hold back, we create unnecessary hostility—much more so than if we just spoke up. **We may be afraid of their reaction, but telling the truth takes less energy than worrying about what *might* happen if we do**.

Being honest doesn't mean being brutal

For us to be heard, we have to learn to speak honestly without malice. Being honest doesn't mean dumping our righteousness and judgments all over our loved ones— *"Hey, don't blame me because you're upset! You wanted me to tell you how I really felt, so stop complaining!"* That kind of antagonism doesn't make it safe for our partner. Sometimes people feel that to be "honest" or "truthful" in our communications gives us permission to say whatever we want in whatever way we want to say it, regardless of the effect it has on another. We think the other person *"...should be able to handle it—after all, I'm being honest with them."*

In reality, we **can** say whatever we want in whatever way we want, but we must also be willing to deal with the consequences. However, when we are in partnership, taking care of our partner and making it easier for him or her to listen with compassion is more important than just blurting out whatever thoughts, judgments, or opinions come to mind. We start to see the impact attacking and accusing have and begin to alter the way we approach sensitive subjects, speaking more appropriately. **We don't compromise the authenticity of our speaking, we simply speak the truth in a way our partners can hear us**. When we practice speaking from our hearts, we become adept at communicating our deepest, heart-felt feelings—not our condemnations.

The best way to begin is by stating our own feelings and experience—resisting the temptation to point the finger at our partners. When we come from a place of accusation, our communications are usually inflammatory and only serve to escalate the problem. We can start training ourselves to speak from our hearts simply by inserting the word "**I**" into sentences that used to be liberally sprinkled with "**You**." Sweeping generalizations will also get us into trouble. Phrases such as: *"You never, you should, you don't, you can't, you won't"* would be best abandoned altogether. Here are some examples of accusatory speaking. As you read, imagine how you would feel if your partner were saying the following to you:

- *"If **you** would just take me seriously once in a while, I might actually want to talk to **you**!"*

- *"**You're** really getting on my nerves! All my friends think **you're** too controlling!"*

- *"I can't believe **you** still feel that way after all this time! What is **your** problem?"*

- *"I don't know why I even bother telling **you** anything—**you never** listen to me!"*

It's only human—the minute we hear *"**You are**..."* instead of *"**I am**..."* we tend to tense up and want to retaliate. When we speak directly from our hearts, it's so much easier for our partner to have compassion for us:

- *"I felt so hurt a moment ago when we were talking."*
- *"I'm so disappointed about what happened."*
- *"I'm frightened and I'm not trusting that you love me."*
- *"I feel angry and I'm having a hard time hearing you."*

Before the words leap out, let's try on what we want to say and see how **we** would feel receiving it. If it feels supportive and caring, go ahead. If not, we can try a different approach—looking over there and remembering that our partner is just as hard on himself or herself as we are on ourself and won't respond well to being attacked. Sometimes we can't help judging—and if we are, we can still take care of our partners by acknowledging we are doing it and apologizing for the pain it causes. Here's an example.

As usual, Francine and I were running late. We left our apartment in San Francisco and then rushed like mad toward our Club meeting. Francine was driving like a New York City cab driver in a hurry, weaving in and out of traffic. Now I'm sitting next to her with my seatbelt practically choking me, bouncing up and down and shouting, *"Watch out for that bus! You're driving too fast! Here comes a red light! You're too close to that car! What the hell do you think you're doing, Francine?!"*

But she doesn't listen, just keeps driving like a maniac. I become angrier and angrier, and she continues to ignore me (understandably, since she's upset and defensive about how critical I'm being!). Suddenly I realize what's happening, and I say, *"I'm so afraid, Francine. I'm scared about the way you're driving and I'm afraid we're going to have an accident and get hurt."* And then, just as suddenly, she hears me and slows down. It was miraculous.

First I saw that she was not able to hear me when I was screaming my anger and judgments and telling her what to do. But when I said I was afraid—when I spoke from my heart—she could hear me instantly. When I told the truth, when I let her know what was underneath my anger, she immediately had compassion for me. Of course she didn't want me to be afraid, so she began driving differently, and apologized for frightening me. After that, I could have compassion for her as well, understanding how much she hated to be late and how important it was for her to get to the meeting on time.

If I hadn't been able to tell the truth about my fear, it would have been so easy to hold onto the anger and the self-righteousness. Many years ago, I wouldn't have shared what I was thinking, I simply would have tried and convicted her:

"Francine doesn't give a damn about me! I'm never going to ride with her again. I'll just get myself to the meetings by leaving early enough to take public transportation. I'm just not going to put my life at risk anymore with her driving! She's insane!"

That kind of thinking used to make **me** insane—I would get terribly upset, fearful, and anxious. But telling the truth calms me down. It becomes clear that Francine is not doing anything to me on purpose—she's just doing what she's doing, and it's my responsibility to let her know how I'm feeling and what I need. I can see what the fear does to me, and I communicate from that place: *"I am afraid. I'm not afraid of you, I'm not angry at you. I'm just afraid."*

When my intention is to speak in this manner, I do myself and Francine a great service. Not only can she hear me, but I strengthen my ability to get in touch with what my heart really wants to say—not just what my mind is telling me.

The cost of not speaking from the heart

When we have a feeling or desire and choose not to voice it, the mischief gains a foothold. If we avoid taking responsibility for our decision, we'll find a way to rationalize why we didn't tell the truth. Now we have to justify why we didn't say what we mean:

- *"If he really loved me, he should be able to tell how I feel."*
- *"She already knows what I want—she just isn't willing to give it to me."*
- *"He's not really interested in what I think anyway."*
- *"If I tell her how I really feel, I'll upset her even more."*

If we choose to not be honest and instead opt for the illusion of comfort with these and other justifications, we're dead right again, believing our stories and excuses instead of dealing with reality. **Our partners don't know what we want because we don't ask for it.** They don't know we're disappointed because we don't tell them, and we blame them for not reading our minds. Sometimes our case against our partner becomes so vivid that we might do something rash. When both men and women hold back important information from one another, the stage is often set for disaster. Consider this letter to a well-known columnist:

Dear Ann Landers,

I was fascinated by that letter from "C in Oregon" who gave such an elaborate explanation when his wife came home and caught him making love to a strange woman. I have written a scenario that is much more believable.

Signed DDD

Dear DDD,

Here's your story—which beat out about 500 others!

Mr. X came home from work early and found his wife in bed with a handsome young man. Just as Mr. X was about to storm out, she stopped him and said, "Before you leave, I'd like you to know how this happened.

"When I was driving home from shopping this afternoon, I hit a hole in the pavement. The hole was filled with water and great blobs of mud splattered all over this man. Without a trace of anger, he looked at me and said, 'What rotten luck. I have a very important meeting this afternoon and just look at me.'

"I told him that I was terribly sorry and offered to clean him up. He seemed grateful and I brought him home.

"He undressed in the bathroom and I handed him the bathrobe I bought you for Christmas a few years ago that you never wear. While his clothes were drying, I gave him lunch—the casserole you missed last night because you decided to go out with the guys after work. He said it was the best home-cooked meal he'd had in

months. I told him it was the first compliment I'd received about my cooking in years.

"We talked while I pressed his shirt and it was wonderful to have a conversation with a man who seemed interested in what I had to say. Suddenly he noticed the ironing board was wobbly. I had asked you a dozen times to fix it, but you were always too busy. The man fixed the ironing board in ten minutes and he actually put the tools away.

"As he was about to leave, he asked with a smile, 'Is there anything else your husband has neglected lately?' And that is the end of my story!"

We may find this amusing, but it points to a very real problem in relationships. When people feel unappreciated and unloved, and there isn't a safe environment to work things out, they may go elsewhere for their comfort and feel justified. In the story in this reader's letter to Ann Landers, what do you suppose hadn't been said in that relationship? What hadn't been heard? You can be sure they weren't trusting they were loved and speaking from the heart. Unfortunately, this drama happens all too often. We withhold our deepest selves from our loved ones and wonder why they don't know us. When we script the scene in our minds, our partner becomes the villain and we're the victim:

- *"I'd tell him the truth, but he wouldn't understand. He's so self-absorbed and stubborn, he doesn't **want** the truth!"*
- *"She doesn't trust me enough to tell me what she really wants, so why should I tell her?"*

- *"I'd say how I feel, except he's always talking about how it's difficult for him to handle emotional outbursts. Why should I bother? It'll just make him insecure again."*

If we withhold ourselves from our partners because we're afraid they'll get upset, we don't give them a chance to love us. If we then lash out at them for not giving us what we need, they probably **will** get upset, and we get to be right—*"See, I knew you couldn't handle me telling you the truth!"* We convince ourselves we know what's real, forgetting that we made up the story in the first place.

Here's an example of how we concoct scenarios and then believe them:

Sam lives way out in the country, and he's driving home at 3:00 AM when his tire goes flat. It's a lonely country road and he's five miles from home, but he's not worried—he knows he has a spare tire. Sam goes to the trunk and opens it but then suddenly realizes that his jack is missing. Where could it be? He thinks for a moment, and then he remembers—he took it out before he went to the hardware store and left it lying on the floor of his garage at home. Now what's he going to do?

Suddenly he remembers that his good friend Larry lives close by. Heartened, he decides to walk to Larry's house—it's only about a half mile away—borrow his jack, walk back to the car, and fix the tire. Then he can swing by Larry's house to return the jack before he heads home.

Happy now, off he goes, walking and thinking of what he's going to say to Larry, when he suddenly says to himself, *"Wait a minute, it's 3:00 AM. What if I wake him up and he gets annoyed and doesn't want to help me?"*

Then he thinks, *"Don't be silly, Larry's my good friend, of course he'll help me."*

"But it's three o'clock in the morning—people aren't usually too thrilled about being awakened in the middle of the night."

He goes on thinking, *"Well, I only want to borrow his jack and besides, it's an emergency. I mean, we've known each other for over twenty years!"*

"Yeah, but what if he's in a bad mood and doesn't want to lend me the jack? Then what am I going to do?"

"Well, who the hell is he to refuse me this little favor! After all, I've gone out of my way for him a hundred times—if he woke me up in the middle of the night with a flat tire, I'd give him my jack! The nerve of this guy! How dare he refuse to help me now when I need him?"

He keeps walking along, talking to himself, until he finally comes to Larry's house. He rings the doorbell, fuming and pacing. Larry finally shuffles to the door, and when he sees Sam, he says, *"Sam, what's happened? Are you okay?"*

And Sam screams at the top of his lungs, *"Larry, you can take your stinking jack and shove it!"* Larry never stood a chance!

This story may be funny, but it's also familiar. We've all done things like this. We believe the story and then interact with our partner in such a way that we end up being right. For instance, we're on our way home, we're late and forgot to call, and we're thinking about how annoyed our partner will be when we arrive. The inner conversation starts and we're off on a mental roller coaster. We're formulating how we're going to explain ourselves and deflect any blame that might come our way. By the time we reach home, our partner doesn't stand a chance either—we've already written the ending!

Saying what we mean

Remember the child who said, *"I'm hungry"*? It's time to start stating our needs instead of asking questions. Often, asking a question is a way we manipulate—not necessarily out of wanting to control others but because we're afraid we're not worthy of getting what we want. We ask a question rather than make a declaration and then get upset when the person gives us an answer we don't like! Not only that, when we ask questions, it's a setup—we give the decision-making power to the other person and then get irritated when they don't see our hidden agenda.

Before asking a question, check in to see how you're feeling and then practice saying what it is you really want:

- *"I'm hungry and I'd like to have dinner."*
- *"We've been working hard all day and I need a break. Let's go see the new French film at the Village Cinema."*
- *"I want to go to bed early tonight. I miss you and want to make love."*
- *"Let's call Jim and Helen and invite them over for dinner Saturday night."*

Our partners might not always respond to these statements the way we would like, but at least we will have expressed ourselves honestly. It's a lot easier to deal with their reaction than if we had covertly hinted and gotten turned down. Both Francine and I have learned to speak up and say what we want, but she's better at it than I am—she's my teacher. I'm still learning how to react truthfully when she says what she wants—sometimes I still say, *"Sure, that's fine"* too quickly before I've thought about whether or not it's really okay with me.

At times I automatically give in to what she wants rather than stand up for myself—it's an old habit left over from my people-pleasing days. Thankfully, Francine's good at making sure we're both taken care of and always wants things to work for both of us. I need to practice remembering to stop and think before I agree to something she's said. That's one of my challenges, and I'm lucky to have a partner who supports me as I learn.

Giving someone a piece of our hearts, not our minds

Another way to describe speaking from our hearts is **speaking our truth**. When we express ourselves authentically, it touches the heart of another human being. The person we are with cannot deny the simple purity of our feelings. When we are genuine, the heart of another naturally opens to us.

We all know how it feels when we are with people who are not being straightforward. We might get a creepy, uneasy feeling—and may not even know why. All we know is we don't feel comfortable and want to end the conversation as quickly as possible. Again, children are our role models here, since they always know when someone is not being sincere with them. A child who is being talked to dishonestly will lose interest, get shy, or scamper away to find a safer place.

We all started out being very good at letting people know exactly how we felt—we didn't censor anything. But gradually we learned that certain emotions—especially anger, sadness, and disappointment—were unpleasant for the people around us. They either wanted us to feel differently, or they crushed our spirits by telling us we couldn't possibly be having those feelings. We adapted quickly to these conditions—or paid the price. I remember a Club member sharing that when she was a child, she was pensive and introspective. Well-intentioned adults were always telling her, *"Smile! You look so much prettier when you smile!"* However, to her, it was as if they were saying, *"...and you look ugly when you don't! Stop being sad and be happy! You're not okay the way you are!"*

After a lifetime of not being heard, we are reluctant to open our hearts and make our wishes known, and with good reason. It hasn't been safe to say how we feel, and our hearts have been broken many times. It is in our partnerships that we can heal these wounds. By trusting we are loved and taking the chance to let our partners know what we want and need, we start to mend the cracks in our hearts.

Speaking from our hearts can be effortless

When we begin speaking from our hearts on a regular basis, it conserves energy. Our conscious mind doesn't have to work so hard—we give it a rest from the endless justifications, excuses, and explanations we thought we had to tack onto everything. It's a relief not to have to make up some crowd-pleasing speech every time we open our mouth. We don't have to monitor and manage every word—we relax and don't feel compelled to ramble. We may speak less, but say much more.

When we speak our hearts to one another, there is no manipulation, no trick, no subterfuge—it's clear as a pond on a windless day. There's nothing lurking under the surface, unseen but felt, causing tension or discomfort. I remember telling my children when they started dating: *"Just tell the truth, and you'll never run out of things to say."* We can put down the burden of being afraid to be who we are.

Speaking from our hearts creates partnership

Being truthful on an ongoing basis helps keep a clean slate between us and our partner. In this environment, any new communication is just that—**new**—not one with emotional residue blowing it out of proportion. When we have conflicts, are they the upsets of the moment or are they frequently recycled ones that keep coming back, crying out to be healed? In the practice of speaking from our hearts, we can keep the current upsets in the present, tending to them before they become another unresolved issue.

When we trust our partners by speaking the truth, we demonstrate our respect for them. We honor their love for us and trust that they're wise and kind enough to listen with compassion. Even if we are worried about their reaction, we must not let this stop us. We may have some fear of sharing our hearts, but we must find the strength to do it anyway. Remember, when we take the leap of faith to communicate, we create the experience of **trusting we are loved**. And, as in all gifts in relationship, it returns to us—when we let our partners into the inner sanctum of our souls, we make it safe for them to do the same.

Each time we trust that we are loved and express our true nature, simply and clearly asking for what we want or saying how we feel, we enrich and sustain all our relationships.

> *If your everyday practice is to open*
> *To all your emotions,*

To all the people you meet,
To all the situations you encounter
Without closing down,
Trusting that you can do that,
Then that will take you as
Far as you can go.
And then you will
Understand all the teachings that
Anyone has ever taught.

—P. Chodron

CHAPTER 6

Creating Safety

*An appropriate human being is one
in whose presence we are safe.*

What does it mean to be safe?

Feeling safe is one of the most basic needs of human beings—it's even more basic than feeling loved. No individual or couple can be completely whole unless safety is present, and yet how many of us truly feel safe in our lives and our relationships?

We all want ourselves and our loved ones to be safe, especially our children. Being safe is the foundation for all emotional and physical health. When we experience safety, we are at peace—able to deal effectively with whatever comes to us.

The definition of **safe** is: ***Secure from danger or harm; affording protection, the condition of being free from injury, unhurt.***

Most of us think of safety in tangible terms—of being physically protected or immune to bodily harm. Without physical safety, there can be no emotional safety, no room for any other of the higher states of awareness, no creativity. If we are being threatened with bodily harm, we have only one purpose—survival.

When we are not in survival mode, we can turn our attention to improving our own lives and the lives of those around us. We naturally want to contribute our talents to others—to share ourselves. We all need to experience that our lives have meaning, that we can make a difference in the world.

Wouldn't we all like to make our Earth a safe place— a place where people, animals, and the environment are not injured or harmed in any way? If I could make one sweeping change just by wishing it, I would make the world safe. In my version of our world, men, women, and children would always be safe—no human being would ever, ever intentionally hurt another.

Of course, because I know human nature, I am aware that the likelihood of that coming true is very small. **But we can do something to make the world a safer place—and it starts with creating safety for those we love**. The humble act of creating safety in our relationships is a fundamental building block in the quest for global safety—and it's something that we can start to do right now, today, with all the people in our lives.

We sit on a bus or subway next to an empty seat, relaxed, reading or looking out the window, safe in our aloneness. But what happens the moment someone sits next to us? Most of us tense up, shrinking back ever so slightly, making sure we don't make eye or physical contact with this **stranger**. When I go for a walk, I say hello to people: *"Good morning! Hello, how are you?"* Most of the time people don't answer me. They shield themselves, lost in their private thoughts, unwilling to respond. Why are we so afraid to simply acknowledge another's greeting? Because it's not safe—even a simple *"hello"* from a stranger seems threatening in a world where people hurt one another every day.

In a world that seems to get more unstable and unpredictable with each passing year, we all are concerned with being physically safe, as we should be. But what I want us to look at together here is this quality of relationship in which each of us is **safe** with one another—not only physically, but also emotionally, mentally, and spiritually.

Creating safety is an ongoing, conscious result of practicing partnership. When we trust that we are loved, listen with compassion, apologize, forgive, and speak from the heart, **the natural outcome is safety**.

Feeling safe in ourselves

When human beings feel safe, we are relaxed, uninhibited, free to express our feelings, play, take risks, and grow. We are not afraid of exposing ourselves or making mistakes. We have no need to protect ourselves from danger, so our energy goes toward self-expression. Safety affords our spirits a haven—a home where we are completely alright and totally loved—**just the way we are**.

When people are safe, their highest selves are expressed, and conversely, when people are threatened, they are at their worst. They will defend themselves, or even willfully attack another. In this regard, we share a common bond with the animal kingdom.

For instance, when is a dog most dangerous? When a dog is afraid, he will understandably defend himself against the enemy, even attacking if necessary. When a dog feels safe, he'll wag his tail and lick our hand, rolling over and exposing his belly (his most vulnerable part!), showing that he trusts us. It's the same with people—human beings who feel safe, loved, and appreciated don't go around mugging each other. When we're safe, we expose our bellies too! When we're safe, we create safety for the people around us. When we are afraid and threatened, we hurt one another.

The Porcupine Analogy

Picture a porcupine, lumbering about in the forest. (Note: A porcupine, contrary to popular belief, does not actually throw its quills. The quills are embedded loosely in the skin, and will come out at the slightest touch if the porcupine relaxes certain muscles.) Our little woodland friend is walking around and looking for food, not bothering anyone. A few curious harmless creatures may stop by to sniff at him, but our porcupine is not the least bit alarmed. His quills are planted securely in his back.

Suddenly, a big, hungry wolf comes out from behind a tree, growling and snarling. He's never encountered a porcupine before and lunges at our little friend, hoping for a meal. The porcupine, terrified, does what he has to do to protect himself—he relaxes his muscles and the quills come loose. The wolf gets a snoutful of painful barbs and then runs, yelping, retreating into the forest. The lesson? **We cause harm to others only when we ourselves feel threatened**. A porcupine who feels safe is nothing to be feared.

When we are safe, we share ourselves with others. The jewel inside shines and shows its true beauty. When I know I'm safe, I speak from my heart—knowing I'll be heard, valued, and appreciated. Basking in the glow of nonjudgment and love, I have permission to truly be myself. When I feel safe, I don't have to try to manage and control people and circumstances to be a certain way—I trust that I'll be able to deal with whatever happens. I feel secure and confident, living in the faith that life is good. I am open to the opportunities for growth that are inherent in every situation that presents itself. I am at peace.

So how can we create this experience of safety?

We are all afraid

The opposite of being safe is being afraid, and yes, **we are all afraid**. However, the first step to creating safety is to realize this. And what are we afraid of? Of the thousands of things human beings fear, I believe at the core for most of us is the fear of being alone— abandoned, rejected, cast out, pushed away, or unwanted. On one level, we are alone because we are unique individuals and separate beings. However, I believe that on a much more significant level, our spirits are one, and we are here to bridge the gap and reconnect with one another.

Although we may try valiantly to do that, many of us continue to feel frustrated, alienated, and unsafe. We are searching for safety—hoping to find it with other people. But what we must realize is that **everyone** is afraid, and those other people are looking for the same safety from **us**. So our first priority is not to **seek safety**—our job is to **create safety for others**, and in doing so, we will **become safe**. As in our previous practices, we've discovered that our authentic healing opportunity lies not in our desire to get compassion, **but in our willingness to have it for others**. Not to hold out for an apology—to offer it. Not to wait for forgiveness—but to forgive.

Some time ago I was speaking to a group of children, ages ten through twelve, at their school in Arizona. I asked them, *"How many of you think that once you become an adult, you will no longer be afraid?"* All the children raised their hands. I told them how sorry I was because, as I said, *"The truth is I am still afraid—in fact, all human beings are afraid. Men, women, and children are all afraid."*

I then told them that it was a sin to frighten another human being, that we don't ever have the right to do that. As I spoke, they all began to look at each other. Then one of the boys requested that I repeat what I said, asking me if it were really true. I assured him it was. Before we parted, each child had taken an oath never to intentionally frighten anyone again. Later I found out that the boy who asked the question was one of the biggest bullies in the class. I left realizing that they'd probably all forget their oath from time to time, but I knew a seed had been planted.

What it means to be afraid

We don't walk around saying, *"Hello, I'm afraid"* to each other. It might be nice if we did. Unfortunately, fear commonly wears three disguises: **anger**, **judgment**, and **withdrawal**.

Most of us are so unaware of how afraid we are that we don't realize how much it runs our lives. We misinterpret what happens in our relationships, not understanding that when we strip away the layers, what's at the bottom is fear.

Sometimes what we are afraid of makes it harder to be with the fears of our loved ones. When my oldest son Kenny was a boy, if he was afraid to try something new, I would get impatient and annoyed. Why? Because: 1) **I was afraid he wouldn't be able to overcome his fear and it would rob him of success later in life,** 2) **I felt like a bad father and blamed myself for transferring my own fears to my children,** and 3) **I felt helpless to support him through to the other side.**

Instead of being compassionate and supportive, my worries manifested as criticism and made it difficult to guide him over his hurdles. How I wish I could have transcended my fears, but at that time I had so little awareness of myself in that way.

What I know now is that children don't need us to be perfect—they need us to be striving for and actively engaged in moving toward our highest goals. We can serve our children when we show them we are human beings, with personal challenges and issues to face. The greatest role modeling we can do for our children is to be committed to rising above our fears and old ways of being. We need to demonstrate to our children that confusing situations in life arise for everyone—that they are opportunities for growth and can be met with courage, integrity, and trust.

Learning to face our fears

Fear is at the foundation of many of the upsets in our day-to-day lives. For instance, the fears beneath the surface of the following statements might be:

- **"How dare you say that to me!"** *(I can't handle my feelings about what you said; it terrifies me.)*
- **"How could you!"** *(You must not really love me, or you wouldn't have done that.)*
- **"I can't believe he got the promotion!"** *(I knew it—they don't really think I'm doing a good job.)*
- **"How could he be late night after night?"** *(Could he be having an affair? What if I'm losing him?)*
- **"Why can't you think of someone other than yourself?"** *(I'm afraid I'm not important to you.)*
- **"How could you let me worry so much?"** *(I guess my feelings don't matter to you anymore. You've stopped loving me.)*

When we're afraid, we may react by getting angry, judging, or withdrawing instead of simply saying, *"I'm afraid."* Why? Because most of us don't feel it is safe to express our fears to one another. And yet we all share so many of the same fears. We're afraid of:

- **Not being loved**
- **Being misunderstood or unjustly accused**
- **Not being successful in our careers or relationships**
- **Being rejected or hurt by a loved one**
- **Not having enough money**
- **Disappointing other people**

- Being exposed as the impostors we think we are
- Losing our job or not living up to our potential
- Making an unforgivable mistake
- Being incompetent
- Looking stupid or foolish
- Being humiliated or embarrassed
- Finding out what people really think about us
- Dying before our time
- Being (or having a loved one) hurt in an accident
- Never finding a partner to grow old with
- Becoming (or having a loved one) seriously ill
- Being abandoned or lonely
- Facing what the future holds for the planet... etc.

We have all had these and other fears, and they are nothing to be ashamed of. The opportunity is in learning to trust our higher power and not let fear rule our lives. An important step is realizing that we don't need to hide our fears from other people.

I have found that one of the best ways to break the ice at a party is to go up to someone new who is standing alone and looking uncomfortable. I introduce myself and then say, *"You know, sometimes I just don't know what to do or say at these kinds of parties—I'm kind of nervous when I don't know a lot of people. What about you?"* This usually creates a sense of relief for the person, because oftentimes they're feeling the same way! We can establish a safe environment when we let others know we are afraid of the same things they are.

We're afraid of our fears

We all share common fears: we're afraid of being misunderstood, not known, not listened to, not appreciated, or just not being good enough. Many of us are also afraid of exposure—afraid people will find out we're frauds or impostors, so we develop an attractive protective skin and try to avoid making mistakes.

Unfortunately we've all gotten so adept at looking good that people buy our act, and by covering up our true feelings, we make it harder for people to get close to us— to know who we really are. After years of pretending, we become so removed from our authentic selves that we become increasingly afraid someone will penetrate our defenses. The paradox is that we sacrifice intimacy and closeness by protecting our vulnerability. We lock up our fears in a trunk, but we also lock up our ability to let ourselves be loved. And who can truly feel safe with someone who hides their heart in a box?

Fear in our closest relationships

How many of us feel totally safe with our partners? Do we trust they are looking out for us or do we fear they will hurt us if they get the chance? How many of us feel safe just being who we are, secure in the knowledge that we are loved? Sometimes it's the people we hoped we'd feel the safest with who are the ones we fear the most. They know our weaknesses—our tender parts. Like an enemy with a well-connected spy network, **we don't trust them to have our best interests at heart**—they know too much about us, and our most sensitive selves are in jeopardy. Instead of trusting that they will be our champion, we live in fear that they will use our vulnerabilities against us to their own advantage—and sometimes they do.

How painful this is! It feels like betrayal, a profound disappointment in something we'd been counting on all our lives—we'd thought we had found our haven from the world, and instead, we live in fear. We become at the mercy of one another's moods—trying to avoid upsetting each other and walking around on eggshells, hoping to stay away from volatile topics and hot issues.

If we are in a relationship such as this, creating safety must be our highest priority. Until we are safe, our relationship will be stunted and we won't be able to receive the gifts it has for us. All our energy goes toward protecting ourselves, and virtually nothing is left for growth and self-expression. When we live in the experience of safety, it becomes our foundation—we build out into the world from that base. Creating safety is about trust—trust that who we are is sufficient, and trust that our partners won't loosen their quills at us when we are at our most vulnerable.

Fear makes us frighten others

Like our friend the porcupine, we endanger others when we are afraid. When I was a parent with young children, I had so many fears. Instead of being able to tell the truth, I covered them up with anger and frustration. My children loved me but were also frightened of me— of the next time I'd get upset or yell at them. I wish I could have told them how afraid I was, and apologized to them for making them afraid. I was stuck in the hopeless loop:

FEAR creating ANGER creating FEAR IN OTHERS

When we are afraid and don't express it, we cram it in the darkest corner of our hearts, hoping it will disappear. We can do this for a little while, but eventually we run out of room. The more afraid we are, the more we feel we must hide our fear. We criticize ourselves for being frightened: *"What's wrong with you? There's nothing to be scared of! What a wimp!"* We dishonor ourselves and our loved ones by not speaking the truth about our fears, and our pain intensifies.

When this happens, we are like powder kegs, ready to blow at the tiniest spark. We are stretched so thin that almost anything can break through the veneer, and when it does, the anger explodes, spewing out and endangering the innocent ones in our midst.

For us to stop this cycle, we must become aware of our fear and tell the truth about it **before** it turns into an inappropriate expression of anger. In our commitment to create safety, we must become conscious of what sets us off and strive to communicate our fears or hurts on an ongoing basis. Before we lash out, we need to stop for that crucial moment and face what's really worrying or frightening us. In creating safety, we take ownership of the misdirected fears that make it unsafe for the people around us.

Another way we protect ourselves is by withdrawing, or taking our love away. When we feel threatened, we often react by pulling inward—not speaking, avoiding contact, even removing ourselves physically by walking out or rejecting our partner's overtures. While this behavior is understandable and easily justified, it can also hurt our loved ones greatly. When we shut them out, keeping them at arm's length and refusing to interact or engage in conversation, our partner often interprets our actions to mean that we don't love him or her.

Of course, when we're trusting we are loved, we're not as susceptible to these thoughts; but the truth is, we need to become conscious of the impact of pulling away and to strive instead to communicate our needs and feelings without withdrawing. It's not always easy to do that when we're hurting, but in the interests of partnership, we must be willing to break through our desire to hide and bring ourselves back for the sake of the greater good.

Fear is not bad

A last word about fear: it's not bad. In fact, fear is our friend and a vital part of our survival. When we listen to our innermost instincts, it can protect us from all kinds of danger.

Fear is also a normal reaction to going beyond our comfort zone and facing something unfamiliar. When we are about to do what we've never done, we naturally experience apprehension—it's normal to be afraid of the unknown. What I'm addressing here is that we need to trust one another enough to tell the truth about what we are afraid of, and have the courage to stop pretending we're not scared. Tell the people who love you how you really feel—when you do, you make it safe for them to tell you.

What is courage?

One of the biggest myths of our culture is that courage is the absence of fear. After all, movie heroes don't spend a lot of time worrying—they have to save the universe, so they jump through the time warp even though they know they'll probably die. Not only do they live, but they save the universe and come away with only a few well-placed scratches. We watch their impressive exploits with awe and perhaps sigh: *"If only I could have that kind of courage."* We think courageous people are those who have conquered their fears, vanquished them, are no longer at the mercy of them. We believe they live their lives unfettered, unburdened by the heavy load of being afraid.

What a fantasy! It'll never happen! We have only to ask the most courageous people in the world to find out that courage is quite the opposite of having no fear:

Courage is being afraid
and doing it anyway.

When we demonstrate courage, we do not let the fear stop us from moving forward; instead we press through the fear and take action. The surprising thing about this is that in the course of taking the action, the fear tends to melt away. Isn't that wonderful? I love that! If we wait around for the fear to subside before we do what we're afraid to do, we'll never get around to it. If we just do it anyway, in the act of doing it, the fear leaves us. Simple, but not easy!

The bravest people are those who are willing to tell the truth about being afraid—not the ones who pretend they're not. Ironically, the people who need to be supported to feel the safest are the ones who act as if they are completely immune to fear. They are terrified to let their guard down even for a moment. They are the most afraid.

When we have the courage to admit our fears, we will find an inner strength and compassion that will enable us to be with others when they are frightened. Why would we say, *"Don't be scared"* or *"There's nothing to be frightened of"* to another human being? Because we're afraid too! However, when we say these things, we must remember that we are denying the experience of another human being, and they are left feeling more alone and scared than they were before. It's okay to be afraid. It's okay to be human. We're all in this together.

Several years ago, a professional marriage counselor joined one of our Men's Clubs. After the first meeting, I asked him, *"Why is a person with your experience and wisdom coming to our club?"* He replied: *"Well, to be honest, I don't know how to practice what I preach."* How courageous of him to tell the truth—in sharing his "weakness" he opened the doorway to growth and healing for himself, and ultimately, to his clients.

In the process of stepping beyond the limits we have set for ourselves, we discover an untapped well of competency and strength. Eleanor Roosevelt said it eloquently: *"We must do the things we think we cannot do."*

How can we create safety?

Start by asking these two questions:

Where do I feel safe in my life?
Where do I feel unsafe?

In thinking about the answers, I would invite you to begin with your home and family—and if you live alone, think about friends, people at your job, or other intimate relationships. Do you feel safe at home? For many of us, the American Dream—a house and yard with a jolly '50s sitcom family—is still etched in our minds when we picture the perfect home.

Those TV families may have had their conflicts and misunderstandings, but with one important distinction: they were always **safe** with one another. Even when the situation was dire, no one was abandoned, abused, humiliated—and whatever the problem was, it got worked out in twenty-three minutes. Although we knew it wasn't realistic, we kept watching, loving that warm and fuzzy glow we'd get, because in our hearts that's the kind of safety we longed for.

How safe do you feel with your family members? How safe do they feel with you? Often we live with hidden anger, resentment, resignation, and frustration. Think of your childhood home—was that a safe environment? Does anything in your present household remind you of the one you grew up in? Some of us are recreating our childhood homes in our present family life; we didn't feel safe then, and we don't feel safe now.

Here are a few more questions to ponder as you read this chapter. Think about the answers in terms of feeling safe to be who you are: being respected, known, loved, listened to with compassion, etc.

- **Where do I feel safe in my life?**
- **Where do I feel unsafe?**
- **Do I feel safe with my partner?**
- **Do I feel safe in my family?**
- **Do I feel safe at my job?**
- **Whom do I feel safe with?**

- **What does this person (or people) do that has made me feel safe?**
- **Whom do I feel unsafe with?**
- **What does this person (or people) do that has made me feel unsafe?**
- **What would have me feel safer in my life/home/job, etc.?**

as well as

- **Who in my life feels safe with me?**
- **What do I do that has this person(s) feel safe?**
- **Who may feel unsafe?**
- **What do I do that has this person(s) feel unsafe?**
- **What can I do to have people feel safer in my presence?**

You don't need to spend a lot of time working on these questions at this point—just take whatever answer comes to mind. This is not homework, it's simply an opportunity to begin an inquiry into this issue and to increase awareness. By the time this chapter is finished, the answers to these questions will have taken on new meaning and depth.

Fear between men and women

Fear is and always has been one of the primary sources of trouble in relationships between men and women. Since puberty, most of us have been given mixed messages about how to play our cards right in relationships. Many of us remember the terror we felt in

elementary school when we had a crush on someone—
"God, I hope they don't find out!" Why not? Because if the
person found out, they would then "have something on
you" and would be in a position of power—we could
get hurt.

As young people, we were often instructed by our
culture to protect ourselves by manipulating other
people. We were told to be mysterious, play hard to get—
don't let him know you really care, keep her guessing.
Why? To wear our hearts on our sleeves put us in
jeopardy. God forbid we should just be who we are and
express our feelings! And then to confuse us further, we
heard other messages: *"Don't pretend to be something you're
not. Be honest, be yourself, don't play games."* What were we
to believe? No one seemed to have the answers, and we
muddled through as best we could.

Now we're adults, and we're still searching for the
answers—books, tapes, and videos about how to solve
the conflicts between men and women are being
published in record numbers, and many have valuable
advice. But the bottom line issue remains the same, and
until this is addressed, no discipline will change it:
**human beings are not emotionally safe with one
another**. Men are afraid of women, women are afraid of
men—unless we start the healing from this most basic
premise, the relationship has no foundation on which
to stand.

Before we find someone to love, we're afraid we'll be
alone. After we find someone, we're still afraid—of losing
their love, falling out of love with them, making a
commitment, finding out what they're really like, talking
about forbidden topics, doing something that'll ruin
everything, etc. We don't trust that we are loved, so we
don't share our fears:

"Will you always love me? Are you going to ask me to marry you? Do I embarrass you? Have you lost respect for me? Do I make you angry? Do you still find me attractive? Do I annoy you? Are you ashamed of me? Do you like my friends? I'm afraid if I commit myself to you, you'll disappoint me, or I'll disappoint you...." All these fears and more haunt us every day, and at such a cost! How can we create a strong and loving partnership when we hide our greatest concerns from our loved one? How can we make it safe for them to share their fears when we hold back from sharing ours?

The good news is, the essence of who we really are is not our fears, but instead the **courage to let ourselves be loved**. In trusting we are loved, we allow others the privilege of honoring our deepest heart-felt feelings, and in doing so, our courage expands. We are actually amazingly strong—strong enough to stop denying we are afraid, strong enough to make another human being safe in our presence.

We must begin by making one another safe—both men and women need to make the commitment to create safety for each other—but I will speak to the men first, since I believe that creating safety for women must be our highest priority.

How men can create safety for women

I believe that when women are safe, we'll all be safe. When women feel safe, they create safety for everyone around them—instinctively reaching out and empowering others. However, when women feel unsafe in any way, all their energy goes toward protecting themselves, so there's very little left over for taking care of others, especially their men! When a woman feels safe in her relationship, her heart opens, seeking ways to support and enhance the lives of her loved ones. Women are the best—they are God's masterpiece. We must make them safe. It is men's most sacred responsibility.

Many of the men I have known and worked with over the years have wondered about this concept, and it's been a provocative topic in the Club meetings! It has been difficult for men to see that if they created safety for women, the women would naturally become more giving—be more affectionate, more loving, more supportive. The men sometimes have trouble seeing this as the logical outcome, especially if they are not feeling particularly taken care of in their relationships. What I tell them is, well, if that's true, it's because the women aren't safe! When women are afraid, they will not be able to express their love because they are trying to protect themselves from us.

I ask men all the time to do whatever they can to make women safe, and then stand back and be in the awesome presence of the outpouring of love, compassion, and understanding that will come to them. When women are safe, men will be safe. And when men are safe, they will have less of a need to lash out with anger and aggression, and the world will be a safer place. This is what I tell the men: **If you want her to make it safe for you, make it safe for her**.

Believe me, I know it's not easy to provide safety for a woman when you're not feeling safe. But please remember that it returns to you—that's the majesty of practicing partnership.

When I want Francine to be safe, my thoughts about myself disappear. I look over there to see what I can do for her.

When we are frightened, we often get angry, and our anger terrifies women. Even if we do not strike out at them, it's in our voices, our faces, our body language—women are innately afraid of violence in any form. Like all living creatures, they are programmed to protect their young, and will either run or defend when they feel threatened.

We need to have the integrity to admit that we take a lot out on our partner. We wouldn't treat a casual business acquaintance the way we sometimes treat our own wife and children. We must stop dishonoring our most cherished ones with this kind of behavior. I ask you, now—**please let yourself be loved**. Create safety for your partner by sharing your fears instead of making her pay for your unexpressed emotions.

How to create safety for a woman

- **Tell her how much you love her, as often as possible.**
- **Apologize if you even *suspect* you've done something to upset her.**
- **Don't frighten or intimidate her.**
- **Tell the truth and trust that you are loved—don't dishonor her or yourself with deception.**
- **Never harm her physically or threaten to do so.**
- **Always share with her what's going on in your life.**
- **Listen to her with compassion.**

- **Ask her what you can do to make her feel more loved and taken care of.**

- **Speak from your heart about your fears, concerns, and desires.**

- **Let her love you the way she wants to love you.**

- **Forgive her.**

- **Make honoring her and her safety your first priority.**

When we are unhappy, our first thought usually is—*"How can I get what I need?"* It's very human, but I am asking us instead to look over there at our partner—and have her needs be of paramount importance. I know it may seem backwards, but I believe **our own salvation** lies in our partner experiencing being loved, appreciated, and safe.

How women can create safety for men

At the risk of sounding contradictory, I will now say that women must also be willing to create safety for men. The general rule of thumb is: somebody has got to make the first move, and we simply can't wait for the other person to do it. It's not enough to be 50% responsible for the relationship working—we've got to be 100% responsible. So let me explain what I think about men and how women can make them safe.

I think men are the craziest of human beings—we need all the love and support you can give us. Make him safe by letting him know that you love him even when he cannot love himself—and be amazed at what happens. Let him walk through the door at night knowing that he is going to be welcomed without criticism or blame. Miracles will occur.

What are men afraid of? Many men are afraid that they aren't sufficient—that they won't be successful. We are so hard on ourselves that we often believe the women we love think we're not good enough either. We blame ourselves if our partner is upset or unhappy, and we frequently don't trust that we are loved, which makes it difficult to share the feelings we may be ashamed of. And when we don't, women frequently interpret it to mean we don't love them. Men tend to feel alone and unsupported, unappreciated and accused. As you can see, men often don't make it easy for ourselves to be loved, and our fears cause us to sometimes become dominating or controlling.

One of the things that men have talked about a lot over the years is how intimidated they become in the presence of a woman who becomes outraged. Many men get paralyzed in the face of that kind of accusation—they don't know what to do, and to have that kind of anger directed at them makes it impossible to listen with compassion. Since they are probably already blaming themselves, when they feel accused by you, they just want to fight back. It makes sense—when a man is being harsh on himself, the last thing he wants is a woman adding insult to injury!

One of the things I tell women who want to create safety for men is to be aware of how your intense criticism affects your partner. Please try to remember that you are speaking to someone who is likely to be very self-critical. Men are so afraid of being wrong, of being a failure. When you are upset, even though you may be right (and you probably are!), your anger is very difficult for him to deal with when it is hurled like a javelin. Believe me, all he wants is to be able to provide you with what you need. Please have the courage to state your complaints and your upsets in a less accusatory manner—I promise that if you can make him safe in this way, he will be able to hear you.

How to create safety for a man

- **Apologize if you even *suspect* you've done something to upset him.**
- **Trust that he loves you. He does!**
- **Listen without trying to analyze or fix him.**
- **Have compassion for him—he's so hard on himself.**
- **Thank him and acknowledge him often for all the big and little things he does.**
- **Forgive him every day.**
- **Put loving him ahead of the need to be right.**
- **Be patient and interested—make it safe for him to share his feelings and fears.**
- **Avoid complaining and nagging with self-righteousness—speak with kindness.**
- **Share your emotions responsibly—tell him how you feel and what you want but avoid making it sound as if it's all his fault.**

Men are often critical of themselves every waking moment—telling themselves what they could have done better, berating themselves for things they haven't achieved, worrying about what's to come, wondering if they're going to be able to provide for you the way they'd like. Your judgment of him won't help—he's judging himself enough for the both of you!

Starting with the people we live with

We can start creating safety in our homes by honoring the people we love. Here is a list of the five practices so far—it is with these tools that we can build the safest and strongest of houses:

1. **Trusting we are loved**
2. **Listening with compassion**
3. **Apologizing**
4. **Forgiving**
5. **Speaking from the heart**

Take a moment to think about what you can do to create more safety in your home. Consider the following questions:

- **How would you like your partner to feel around you?**
- **What does he or she do that allows you to feel safe?**
- **What does he or she do that makes you feel unsafe?**
- **What does your partner really need from you right now?**
- **What does your partner need from you when they are upset or frightened?**

- **What can you do today to make your partner feel safer with you?**
- **How can making your partner feel safe lead to you feeling safe?**

There is tremendous power in taking a stand, in making statements that declare our intentions in life:

I will make him safe in my presence.

I will make her safe in my presence.

When we speak our heart's voice into the world, miracles happen. We find ourselves automatically doing and saying the appropriate things to effect positive change.

I saw a magazine cartoon once in which a wife calls her husband's office after he's left home for work and says to his secretary, *"Just wanted to warn you—I forgot to give him his good-bye kiss."* The wife knows that he's going to be in a foul mood and she wants to alert everyone to be prepared. We've all experienced the pain of facing another demanding day after an unexpected fight with our partner.

It's unpleasant and stressful, but people muster the strength to do it every day. However, it takes a toll on us, because we are trying to build on a weakened foundation and the whole structure suffers. Imagine what it could be like if our homes were truly the havens of safety we always dreamed of. Isn't that worth working for? We must do whatever we can to make our homes safe. I believe that what we learn about creating safety we must also bring out into our schools and communities—for our children's sakes.

I am safe with Francine. This does not mean that I never get upset, or that she doesn't get angry with me, or we don't have issues to deal with. That is an integral part of living with another person. She makes it safe for me, because I know that whatever happens, she loves me absolutely and is completely committed to me and my well-being.

Knowing that I'm safe in my home, I experience a profound sensation of serenity. I breathe a sigh of relief—*"I'm OK. I'm going to be alright. Everything's going to be fine. Whatever happens to me, to us, I am safe."*

Francine is my best friend, my dearest one, my full and equal partner. She takes care of me, her love heals me, and her compassion keeps me well. I promise that you can have this experience with your loved one. When you and your partner are safe with one another, you give each other the most precious gift—the knowledge that no matter what happens, **you are loved**.

Creating safety is a gift from God

When we are able to look over there and see another human being, realizing that they are just as afraid as we are, that they have the same fears and struggles, we become selfless. Our compassion reveals itself and our job is clear: we are here to make people safe in our presence, to give them permission to express themselves without fear. In every interaction both small and significant, we must come from a place of creating safety. In any given situation, we can ask ourselves: *"What can I do to have this other person feel safe right now?"*

We have the power to create safety with everyone we meet at any time. What an experience—to live in the grace of our essential oneness—to know that we are not alone in this experience of being human. At the heart of it, to create safety is to **trust**: trust in ourselves, trust that we are loved, trust in God. It's about living in a shelter called partnership, an exquisitely benevolent place where we are actively committed to the emotional and physical welfare of the people in our lives, as they are to ours.

When I forget I am loved . . . I am afraid.
When I remember I am loved . . . I am safe.
When I listen I am loved . . . You are safe.
When I trust that I am loved . . . We are safe.

Living with another person successfully continues to be our most potent training ground. Everything that is splendid in human beings comes forth when we are safe. We do our finest work, are at peak creative potential, express ourselves with kindness. Making it safe for others is more than a moral imperative—it is a homecoming to God's grace. When people are safe with us, we will manifest our most divine nature, and life will be blessed beyond measure.

Please remember to say thank you to the people who keep you safe.

CHAPTER 7

Creating Intimacy: Include Your Partner

*Trust creates intimacy,
intimacy creates trust.*

Do we want intimacy?

When I ask people if they want more intimacy in their relationships, they usually say yes. Yet they often have some painful associations and fears about it as well. Why? How can that kind of familiarity and closeness be frightening? Simple—because we feel alone in our lives, afraid of exposing our vulnerability. We've all been hurt before, but because what we really want is true intimacy, most of us are still willing to take the risk again and again. We are not gluttons for punishment; what we are is committed to loving and being loved—that's why we keep coming back, hoping it will be different this time.

Many of us complain that we don't have intimate relationships and yet, when we are faced with the reality of what it takes to have intimacy, we're gone so fast we leave a trail of smoke. Does it make sense to fear or resist that which we want and need? It does if we're a human being! So let's look together at what I mean by intimacy and then at the pathway toward creating it: **inclusion**.

Intimacy has a significant purpose in the development of a whole individual. If we live alone, for whatever reason, we may be lonely—but we are also somewhat protected from the kinds of experiences that arise only when we live with another. I believe that sharing our lives with someone else affords us with unique opportunities to discover our true selves and our fullest potential.

We can heal our relationships with ourselves through our intimate relationships. Being close to another person brings up most of the issues we need to deal with in order to move forward in our growth process. By handling whatever comes up in the context of being intimate, we are being guided by one of nature's greatest catalysts— the art of facing ourselves in the presence of another human being. Whatever our challenges may be, intimate relationships are tailor-made to assist us in discovering who we are and becoming our most realized selves.

How do we create intimacy?

Intimacy is the natural result of **creating safety**. When we are intimate with another, we trust that we are loved. We don't hesitate to share our feelings, thoughts, and concerns—because we know that the other person has the same commitment we do to the health and well-being of the relationship. We can expose even our most delicate souls, confident that our partner is looking out for us.

Sometimes we feel disconnected and alienated from everyone. We can't believe that someone else could understand or know us that deeply—and even if they could see inside, would they still love us? When we are in this dilemma, it looks like a bad idea to risk being known—and yet, to have true intimacy we must take this leap of faith. For us to create partnership in relationship, we need to learn to **include others** in our lives.

What is inclusion? Our dictionary definition says **include** means: *To become a part of.* Isn't that what we want, to become a part of another person's life, experience and heart—and have them be a part of ours? When we don't feel included, we often translate that to mean that we are not loved. In that place of rejection, we frequently push the other person away as a means of defending ourselves.

I remember when I was a kid growing up in New York City, sometimes the older boys wouldn't include the younger kids in their games. So we (the younger boys) would swagger around and act tough, as if we didn't care. God forbid we should let them know how hurt we were—if we did, they'd taunt and tease us, call us crybabies. So we pretended we didn't really want to be with them anyway. *"Well, we don't want to play with you, either!"* we'd say, and walk off, heads held high. The interesting thing was that everyone knew it was just a big bluff—the big kids knew and so did we. But we never spoke about it—it was too embarrassing to admit our feelings were hurt.

As children living in poverty, we quickly learned the dangers of letting someone know how we really felt—we had to grow up fast just to survive. How sad it was for us, kids acting like little grownups, robbed of the purity of young children—that willingness children have to say what they want and tell the truth.

However, eventually all of us learn that it's not safe to expose our hearts. We're misunderstood, lied to, humiliated and hurt, so by the time we become adults, we've got ourselves protected and packaged, and, we hope, impervious to pain. Unfortunately, by building these walls, we also keep out the things we want the most—to be a part of, to be intimate with, another person.

Few of us had the freedom to be open and honest with others. Most of us learned in childhood that it wasn't okay to talk about what was going on at home. Remember hearing from your parents that good children didn't share family secrets? *"What happens here is nobody's business but our own!"* We all know what damage this has done—we learned to pretend, keep our mouths shut, suppress our natural need to share ourselves with others. No wonder we're often ashamed to speak truthfully about what we think and feel.

Often when we finally do get up the courage to share our thoughts and opinions, we hope people will agree with us or we wonder why we bothered. When I was a boy, I used to go to the movies with my friends a lot. Afterward I'd get excited and want to tell them what I thought about the film, but most of the time they disagreed with me, looking at me like I was an idiot and had missed the whole point. Finally I felt so stupid, I just stopped telling them what I thought, and instead, listened to them rattle on, feeling resentful and angry. Eventually I stopped associating with them altogether. I took myself away rather than confront them with a difference of opinion.

It may not be easy to accept that everyone's not going to agree with or like what we have to say when we start revealing our true selves. However, we strengthen our ability to let ourselves be loved each time we trust enough to unmask our hearts.

The ancient Chinese philosopher Lao Tzu said, *"He who does not trust enough will not be trusted."* I've found this to be so true—it's much more difficult to trust someone who won't trust me! And yet, at the same time, I have compassion for that, because we all have legitimate reasons not to trust one another. Just as with compassion and creating safety, we cannot wait for the other person to begin the dance. If you want someone to include you, include them! One of the ways we create intimacy is by **being intimate**. It's a paradox! Simple, but not easy!

Including our partners

Until we become comfortable trusting we are loved, we may feel safe telling our partners only about our opinions and points of view—not our darkest fears and loftiest dreams. Even then, we hope that they will agree with us and not challenge what we say. After all, isn't that what true love is? Someone who likes us so much that they'll never contradict us and never get upset?

We think intimacy is being so close that we finish each other's sentences, laugh at all the same jokes, want all the same things—in effect, we are an extension of one another. We may have some of this in our relationships in the beginning when romantic love is in full bloom, but eventually we're going to have conflict. That's when the challenge of true intimacy starts. Some might say the honeymoon is over. I say, perhaps, but the relationship has just begun!

Instead of including our partners in our worries and concerns and being really intimate with them, we often pretend that we're okay—or we get angry and sullen, hoping they'll get the hint and ask us what's wrong. We're afraid that we won't be safe in their hands and don't trust that they'd understand and appreciate what we're going through. But what are we really afraid of— and are these fears valid?

Of course we will, in our lifetimes, meet people who are so wounded themselves that they are cruel and unkind. Yes, it is unwise to share our most vulnerable selves with those people. But our partner, our dearest friends, our family members—these are the people with whom we want true intimacy, and it is in these relationships where we can practice trusting we are loved.

What stops us from including our partner?

It might be easy if you're just talking about things, other people, politics, or day-to-day plans. But what about the subjects you're afraid to bring up, the things you're afraid to say?

Sometimes we can be more intimate with friends than with the closest person in our life. Why? Because we have so much at stake, so much to lose if they leave us or withdraw their love. Some people have told me about how they rehearse every word before they tell their partner anything important, wanting to make sure they say the right thing. Others feel like they have to tiptoe around, fearful of their partner's reactions, avoiding confrontation, hoping not to rock the boat. Well, guess what? **We *will* rock the boat**! That's what we do! We can't help it—we're human, and we can't spend our lives constantly navigating around the possibility that we might upset another person. When we're intimate, we find out that we're actually in the same boat together.

Women's friendships have traditionally been more intimate than men's—that makes sense, since women have been given more encouragement throughout their lives to connect emotionally. When men are feeling close with one another, they often talk about sports, their jobs, their health, but find it difficult to go beyond that invisible wall. We have a running joke in the Men's Clubs—if you ask a man how he feels, he'll say:

> *"I feel like watching television."*
> *"I feel like having a beer."*
> *"I feel like taking a nap."*

Certainly that's the way I was for most of my life. My main aim was to get people to like me—so I developed a "Lewie" that people would like. I certainly didn't want anyone to know about the "Lewie" who was lonely and terrified of being rejected. I put on a great act—everyone thought I was confident and carefree—but it cost me the gift of being intimate, of being known by another person. It all started when I was thirteen, just beginning my adolescence, when it was even more important than ever to be accepted.

I was born with my right eye crossed, looking at my nose, and I lived like this through my early childhood until a generous, angelic woman arranged an operation for me when I was thirteen. Before that, I was singled out as somewhat of a freak. I was ridiculed when I played baseball. If someone else dropped the ball, the kids would say, *"It's all right, better luck next time."* But if I didn't catch it, they'd say meanly, *"Whadya expect? He's Cockeyed Lewie!"*

After I had recovered from the operation, I remember standing in front of a large cracked mirror in my mother's bedroom. I felt much better about how I looked, but I was still very insecure. I thought, *"If I could just be a certain way, people would like me."* So I said to the kid in the mirror:

"Now, listen to me. If you want to be popular, you're going to have to stop being afraid. You'll have to learn to act clever and smart and tell jokes. People like entertainers—so you need to learn to sing, dance, and make them laugh so they'll want you around."

And so I did. I learned to do all these things and eventually became quite a smooth talker. I was quick and funny and used that to survive and hide my desire to be liked. I became so adept at being this adorable Lewie that no one suspected how afraid I was—and the more I did this, the more I had to make sure no one found out what was really underneath. Much later in life, as I came to know many people intimately, I discovered that most of us developed ways to keep other people from getting too close, to keep them from finding out how terrified we were. Who in your life do you know puts up a convincing front but secretly fears that he or she is not good enough?

Men tend to hold their cards close to their vests, afraid to expose them to anyone. Paradoxically, women often misinterpret that behavior to mean the men don't love them. We must honor women by letting them into our hearts. When we can override our natural tendency to keep everything inside and allow our partner to know what's going on, we create safety and let her love us.

Very few of us had role models who could show us how to be intimate. Did your parents trust each other?

Were they a partnership? Were they intimate? Try as we may to be better than our parents at living this life, they were our first models and we can't help being affected by them. Now that we are adults, we can have compassion for them, forgive them, and let go of the behaviors that keep us separate from one another.

The first step

The first step in learning to include our partner is to become aware of how we don't include them. Perhaps early in the relationship we were brave and told them a secret, special dream or fantasy and then were badly hurt when they betrayed our trust in some way. They may have invalidated us or just didn't listen. Saddened and disappointed by the person we wanted most to honor us, we decided that perhaps it wasn't safe to tell them **everything**. Bit by bit, we began to censor ourselves. We didn't want to take the chance of being hurt, and before long, we had a list of topics that we wouldn't talk to them about.

The irony of it is that when we build the fortress to keep out the dragons, we keep out all the love and light too. In our journey toward partnership, we are faced each day with this question:

"Am I willing to give up everything I think I know for the possibility of what could be?"

This is a new day. It's time to rebuild the trust that may have been breached between ourselves and our partner. It's time to acknowledge how we may have been holding back. It's time to include our partner in our happiness, disappointments, expectations, and dreams.

Share your fears and ask your partner to embrace you. Share your ideas and hopes for the future and ask him or her to support you. Say what you've been unwilling or afraid to say. Give your partner the opportunity to see all of you and the chance to be trustworthy. It's painful for people when we keep the door to our hearts bolted—and we may be pleasantly surprised at how thrilled they are to finally be allowed into the inner sanctum.

When people don't have all the information, they're tempted to fill in the blanks themselves—and when they do, it's usually much worse than the truth. They tend to make up their own interpretation of what we're thinking or why we're being a certain way—and think it's real! Give yourself and your partner a break from the hallucinations—include them!

One wife in the Women's Club was having a difficult time with her husband. He was a busy executive, running his own business as well as heading up a big charity. He was under enormous strain and had virtually stopped talking—only offering curt replies to her questions.

It got worse—he began being condescending and rude. Even though she was extremely hurt, she kept attempting to excuse his behavior because of the stress he was under. One day she finally blew up. She'd run out of excuses, and the truth is, it was a blessing. She said, *"I'm all out of patience—I don't deserve to be treated like this! I don't care anymore about your problems and the pressures of your job—I've had enough!"* This outburst initially alarmed him, but it was a wake-up call and jolted him out of his unconsciousness. Abruptly he was being called forth to come out of his self-absorbed reverie and look over there at her! What a service she did them both that day! Thank God for the courage of women!

But what if she hadn't included him? Odds are she would have continued to retreat into her pain, taking herself away more and more. If she never had told him how she really felt, she most likely would have become resigned about the future. She might have decided after awhile that it wasn't worth it, and eventually chosen to leave the relationship—to anyone on the outside looking in, she would have been completely justified. It's tragic when love becomes eclipsed by that which we are unwilling to communicate to one another—what a loss.

Relationships usually don't die because of what's said—they die because of what's *not* said.

This story has a happy ending: because she did include him, they began having productive conversations. She realized that his behavior was a sign of extreme distress, that his demons were tormenting him intensely. Although his anger and frustration were directed **toward** her, she now knew it actually had nothing to do **with** her, so she stopped taking it personally and was able to have compassion for him. He then apologized profusely for taking all of it out on the person he loved the most and for all the anguish he had caused.

His holding back had hurt her immensely, so he began including her in what was happening with him and his business—sharing the details and telling her when he was worried and confused. The more he included her about his concerns, the less stress he had to deal with, and the more she felt included, the more compassion she had. One of the things he realized is that he didn't want to burden her with his problems until he had a solution— after he'd figured it all out, he thought, **then** he'd include her!

We have all done this and it's understandable, but this kind of thinking has historically led to a great deal of mischief. Not only do we shoulder the burden alone, but our partner senses we're closing down and feels shut out. **We must remember that we don't always have to present our partner with fully fleshed-out plans and concepts—we just need to include him or her in wherever we are in our process.** These two fine people came to a crossroads in their relationship and learned a pivotal lesson. Their partnership has become one of the strongest I've ever seen between a man and a woman.

Share yourself with those who love you

We've all seen poignant films about people who never found the courage to express their love to someone—then that person eventually marries someone else, dies, or something else stands in their way. They've lost their chance, and we grieve for them the way we grieve for the times we have not shared our love. It's so sad—many people don't even know how to say the words, *"I love you."* Children still grow up today never having heard that from their parents. I can hardly believe it, but it's true.

It often takes a time of severe illness or other family crisis before we give ourselves liberty to tell the truth to someone dear. Please don't wait for an emergency to include your loved ones. Don't save it just for special occasions. Express all of it—your thoughts, fears, and love on a daily basis. **Life is happening now—each moment is priceless.**

When we include our partners, it cuts through all the pretense. We can relax because we don't need to hide anymore. How many times have we tried to tough it out alone, thinking, "*No one really cares, anyway, I'll have to deal with this on my own....*" To believe this creates needless suffering—we take ourselves away, withdraw from our partner, exclude them from the privilege of truly being part of us. Recreate the connection you had with your partner in the beginning—let him or her know who you are again. I promise you, not only will the relationship survive, it will prosper!

We are not meant to be alone

We were put on this earth to be with one another. We are individuals, but we were not meant to be wrapped up in our own personal cocoons forever—sooner or later we've got to come out and take flight. When we include our partner in our fears, concerns, and disappointments, we remember we're not alone.

Share your greatest wishes, ambitions, and fantasies with your partner. Have the courage to reveal the secrets of your heart. In the safety and sanctity of our partnerships, we create wondrous deeds and go beyond self-imposed limitations. The more intimate we are with our partner, the more adept we become at sharing our wholeness with others.

You're safe with your partner—this is the one who loves you and comes home to you every night. Trust that you are loved. Let them love you. We were not meant to be alone in this life. We were put here to trust one another and become a part of one another. Look over there at this person who loves you and let them into your heart. I guarantee, they will let you into theirs.

CHAPTER 8

Handling Upsets Responsibly

*Upsets are nature's way of telling us
attention must be paid.*

Upsets are universal

Many of us are walking upsets, waiting to happen. If you watch people as you go through your day—as you work, shop, run errands, you may wonder what I mean. I'm not referring to couples standing on the street corner shouting at each other. Occasionally we see people who are visibly upset with one another, but that's the exception.

What I'm talking about is more subtle. If we observe people closely, we can see the tell-tale signs in some of them—the remnants of pain etched in their faces, the lines of resentment around their eyes, the lips set in resignation. Our culture is based on people feeling good and being happy—all we have to do is look at magazine covers and television commercials to see how much fun we should be having. We attempt to steer clear of potentially upsetting situations and people, navigating around them as best we can. We've all expended lots of energy avoiding being upset, treating certain people as we would an unwanted virus.

What I've noticed is that being upset is a normal part of the human experience and one which we consistently invalidate. Most of us are still attempting to get to that place where we've got all our ducks in a row and don't get upset anymore. We deny our humanity every day when we think being upset indicates something is wrong with us or our partner. **The truth is, trying to avoid being upset can be very upsetting**! When we do this, we tend to get upset even more; and more importantly, we squander the valuable lessons the upset has to teach us.

One important distinction I wish to make right away is that **upsets are not bad**. They are part of life and the human condition. In fact, they are opportunities for growth. Just as a burning sensation is nature's way of letting us know that we've put our hand too close to the fire, upsets are a way the universe informs us that attention must be paid. I believe each and every upset we have is just God's way of offering us the next task at hand; and if we can be receptive to it, we can benefit tremendously. Upsets are a spotlight focusing our vision on what needs to be healed—and if we take the opportunity, they can be a pathway to sanity and wholeness. **The measure of a healthy relationship is not necessarily whether or not upsets occur, but how quickly we can recover from them, enhanced and enriched by their healing lessons**.

I've spent much of my life being upset. For most of my adult life I was performing live shows two or three times a week. It was easy for me to be on stage—no one knew my history or problems, I could say and do whatever I wanted, I could display my greatness and win everyone's love. However, off-stage I was either walking around pretending nothing bothered me, or at home taking out my frustrations on my family.

The minute I stepped on stage, all my fear dissolved and I felt powerful, free, completely at ease. I convinced myself that only my audience appreciated me—*"It's my family who doesn't know who I am,"* I thought. It wasn't until much later that I realized this was a self-fulfilling prophecy I had invented and that it was not accurate. However, as long as I believed it, I was a terror at home—intimidating and easily angered. It took most of my adulthood to get to the place where I felt known and could take good care of the people I loved. I've developed a profound trust in the process of life, and the things that used to upset me don't have the same power anymore.

The only place I really get upset anymore is in my relationship with Francine. That is the way it is for most of us. The more intimate the relationship, the more there is at stake and the stronger the emotional reaction. But even with Francine, I'm handling it better—I'm proud of myself for how much I've grown, and excited about continuing to learn to be a loving human being.

The majority of my upsets occur when I forget that she loves me: I don't think she's listening to me, she interrupts me and I feel that she doesn't care about what I'm saying, or she says something I don't like and I decide I'm not important to her. When I forget that I am loved by Francine, I am ripe for an upset. We all need to become conscious of what causes most of our upsets, since a lot of them seem to follow similar patterns.

We don't know how to deal with anger

Anger is probably the most unpopular of emotions, and with good reason. In its most explosive incarnations, it has caused people to do great harm. But anger doesn't appear in a vacuum. When a human being is hurt, either physically or emotionally, the most natural reaction is a desire to retaliate. As we begin to heal ourselves in the spirit of partnership, we must remember that at the foundation of anger is hurt and fear.

Anger can take many forms. It isn't always screaming and yelling. Often, anger takes the form of hostile silence or sarcastic remarks aimed directly at our hearts. As upsets go, it can be much easier to deal with sadness or even disappointment. Anger is unpredictable and therefore much more troublesome.

When we were young, our childish anger was usually met with resistance by the adults in our lives. An angry child is undesirable and must be dealt with quickly and sternly! Our parents wanted us to calm down, go to our room until we could treat them with respect, count to ten before we spoke. It was implied in many ways that anger was not acceptable, that we must learn to control it—anger was unpleasant, scary, and unattractive. No surprise that many of us have deep wells of unexpressed rage. Some of us live with the worry that either we or our loved ones will "lose our tempers" and the fury will come gushing out.

Unfortunately, since many of us have not been taught how to be angry without being abusive, our fears are justified. I believe that we first must have compassion for our anger, and forgive ourselves for the damage we've done by expressing it inappropriately. We must create safety in our relationships so that anger has a place to come forth and be honored, just as other emotions do.

To begin with, we need to stop giving anger such a bad rap and allow it **to be**. When we do that, we will find that much of its force is diminished. When anger has permission to just exist without invalidation, it doesn't need to puff itself up in order to be heard—it can simply be communicated, without having to knock down trees and buildings in its wake. We must generate compassion for those of us who are angry—and be committed to finding ways of expressing our anger so that we do not continue wounding one another.

Why do we get upset?

When I'm already angry at myself, it's easy to interpret something Francine does or says as criticism. If we can stop to look at what is really upsetting us, it's frequently our own self-judgments being manifested in our partners.

One Sunday at our home in San Francisco, Francine and I decided to take a day off. We'd been busy for many weeks, traveling, going to Club meetings—finally we were going to have some time to ourselves. We planned a special day eating our favorite foods, watching movies on TV, and making love. I was so looking forward to our being together.

There was a drought in the city, and people were being asked to conserve water. That morning, I was washing my socks in the bathroom sink, and Francine peeked in as she walked by and said good-naturedly, *"Too much water!"*

Well, I became furious immediately. I threw my socks into the sink, stormed out into the bedroom, and yelled: *"How dare you say that to me? What else do you have to criticize me for today? Is this the way you talk to me first thing in the morning? Well, I don't give a damn about you, and you're the last person I want to spend time with—I don't want to have anything to do with you. I don't need you or this relationship!"*

I was a raving maniac. And God bless Francine, she just listened to me with compassion and then said, *"Lewie, I'm sorry you're upset, but I won't have that. This is our day together and we've been planning it for a long time. Today is our only time to be together, and this is just not acceptable to me."*

I didn't say anything, but I walked into the closet and started to get dressed. Then I thought: *"What happened, Lewie? What made you get so angry? Here you were, looking forward to this special day with your wife and the next second you're screaming and refusing to have anything to do with her! What happened?"*

Suddenly I remembered that in the precise moment before Francine made the remark, I had said to myself, *"Too much water, Lewie."* I had judged myself, and when she judged me for the same thing, I became outraged. How dare she criticize me! I went to her and immediately apologized. She forgave me, and we had the most delightful day together.

We blame ourselves for big and little things all the time; we're so used to it that we hardly notice. But let the very same judgment come out of our partner's mouth and we want revenge! It's so painful to have our own self-criticism mirrored by another. We're so human! As we grow and learn in our partnerships, handling upsets responsibly means, in part, becoming aware that **we** are frequently the source of our upset—and since the only behavior we can change is our own, we need to be willing to look at ourselves and own that.

As we become more responsible for our upsets and their effect on others, it's important to become conscious of how they start. We can then see how **we're** part of the dynamic—it's not just our partner's shortcomings. We need to look at ourselves and take ownership of what **we've** made up, what **we've** been unwilling to say, what expectations **we've** become attached to. As we all know too well, it's easy to place all the blame on someone else; however, in creating partnership we need to be dedicated to noticing how we may be contributing to the situation.

Anatomy of an upset

The more we become aware of what's at the heart of our upsets, the more we will react and respond to our partner in positive ways.

Many years ago, one of my teachers taught me that most of our upsets begin with one or more of the following three circumstances:

1. **An unfulfilled expectation**
2. **A thwarted intention**
3. **An undelivered communication**

Think about it for a moment—consider something that's been upsetting you recently. Which one (or more) of the three circumstances above best describes what occurred before your upset?

When we hope that something will turn out a certain way and it doesn't, we may be disappointed—**an unfulfilled expectation**.

When someone or something keeps us from doing what we want to do, we might become frustrated or angry—**a thwarted intention**.

When we don't say what we really want to say or don't tell the truth, it can cause pain for ourselves and/or our partners—**an undelivered communication**.

Upsets are part of being with people

When we live with someone and share everything from sex to child rearing to home ownership, there are many opportunities for upsets. In each of the following scenarios, think about what might be going on under the surface between you and your partner in terms of thwarted intentions, unfulfilled expectations, and undelivered communications. Sometimes these situations won't bother us at all; at other times, they can be infuriating!

- **You're washing the dishes and just as you finish, your partner brings in dirty dishes and throws them in the sink.**

- **Your partner leaves every light burning in the house even after you've mentioned the high electric bill over and over again.**

- **Your partner's always nagging you to leave on time when going out to meet friends, but is always late when it's just the two of you.**

- **He likes to get up early; you like to stay up late.**

- She likes to go to parties; you'd prefer to stay home and watch videos.

- He faults you for spending too much on groceries, and then goes out and buys a piece of expensive electronic equipment because "he really needs it."

- She gets mad at you for giving her advice when she doesn't want it, then turns around and does the same thing.

- He complains that you're not sexually assertive enough, and then when you do reach out, he pulls away and says he doesn't feel like it....

This list could go on forever. When we live with another human being we're constantly confronted with the reality of *"You're not ME!"* Some of us are perpetually annoyed with that one—we keep expecting our partners to do/think/act/feel the way we do, and are constantly disappointed when they don't. **When we live in partnership, we have respect for the differences and honor our partner's choices and needs as we do our own.**

I've heard single folks wishing they could be married and married people longing for the simple days of being single. I've never been without the companionship of a woman for very long in my life, but I know some people who, by choice, don't want to have an exclusive relationship. Living with another human being is my preference, and because I choose that, it also means I will be continuously intruded upon and called forth to grow. **The bottom line is: no one else is ever going to be exactly like us, or always do things precisely the way we want them done.**

We can either complain about it and wish it weren't that way, or we can have respect for the differences and accept the fact that to live with someone means we will get upset sometimes by what they do or don't do. To be in partnership means we must be vigilant to not fall into the trap of blaming our partner for everything. Whenever we are interacting with another person, the potential for an upset exists. How much value we get out of our upsets is determined by how willing we are to include and embrace them.

What's really happening?

As soon as I feel an upset coming on with Francine, I try to step back and isolate what happened to trigger it. If I can do that, I may be able to prevent it from escalating, and I let her know right away what occurred. Sometimes, however, if my imagination is working overtime, I add significance to what Francine says or does, and I'm off and running. We all do this, and sometimes it can grip us until we realize what's really happening. Here's an example.

I had been out of town for about three weeks. When I arrived home about 2:00 AM, Francine was sound asleep. I showered, got into bed, snuggled up, and put my arms around her, so glad to be home again. Suddenly, she jabbed her elbow into me and said grumpily, *"I'm sleeping!"* Immediately hurt and angry, I threw off the covers and stalked into the kitchen, muttering to myself:

"I've been away for three weeks and she doesn't have any consideration for me. Who the hell needs this anyway? If this is the way it's going to be, then what the hell do I need to come home for? Why do I bother? Who cares!"

I opened the refrigerator, took out a cold soda, and went into the living room to watch television. After sitting there for only a few moments, I suddenly said to myself, "*What the hell am I doing, sitting here watching television naked in the middle of the night when I want to be in bed with my wife?*" Then I realized that the only thing Francine had said was, "*I'm sleeping.*" She didn't say, "*I don't love you anymore and I never want to see you again.*" I had made up this whole story about how she didn't want me to touch her, wasn't glad to have me home, and didn't care about me. I also remembered that I needed to have compassion for her, to put myself in her place, and imagine how I might react if I'd been awakened suddenly out of a sound sleep at 2:15 in the morning.

Still naked, but much more enlightened, I went back into the kitchen. I toasted an English muffin and prepared some tuna salad, making one of Francine's most beloved snacks. I placed the tuna mixture on the muffins and melted cheese on top. Then I brewed some fresh coffee and fixed it just the way she likes it. I found a tray, and on it carefully arranged a linen napkin, pepper mill, coffee, the tuna melt and tableware, and brought it into the bedroom. I knelt down beside Francine and gently said, "*Francine, my sweetheart, I have a surprise for you.*"

She opened her eyes, smelled the fresh coffee, and was instantly awake. I said, "*Would you like a little something to eat? I made you a tuna melt.*"

And Francine sat up and said, "*Oh, Lewie, this is great!*" We cuddled and talked about my trip while she ate her tuna melt and we enjoyed our little impromptu party immensely. I was so proud of myself that I could let go of the upset and instead trust that Francine loved me.

Basically I believe we get upset with our partners because:

1. **We don't trust that we are loved.**
2. **We don't listen with compassion.**
3. **We add meaning to what's said to us and think it's true.**

I believe it is crucial that we acknowledge our part in each and every upset with our partner—we must train ourselves to look first at our own selves and relinquish blame.

Handling upsets responsibly

Here's a review of some of the previous practices and how they relate to upsets:

Speaking from our hearts

When we speak from our hearts, we've done everything we can to ensure that our partner knows the truth about how we feel. If we don't tell the whole truth, how can we possibly expect them to fully appreciate our experience? Partnership is a place to experiment with being authentic. We don't need to be diplomatic or covert to win the love of our partner. When we are upset, we must trust them enough to be genuine with our requests and our grievances.

Sometimes when we are at an impasse and feel boxed in, simply saying what's true for us can be the key to moving forward. If we can speak to our experience of being where we are **now**, we create the possibility for movement. The more we deny our experience, the more we tend to stay stuck. How many times have we said we're okay when we weren't, and regretted it? Upsets give us the opportunity to practice speaking the absolute truth and acknowledging what is:

If we're in the middle of an argument and it's going nowhere:

"I don't feel safe right now. I know you're not my enemy, but for some reason, I feel unsafe and defensive. I want to work this out, but I feel we need to stop for a moment and be willing to look at what we can do to create safety."

Instead of giving our partners the silent treatment:

"I'm really upset and I don't know what to do or say. I know you like to just plow through and stick with it, but I just don't feel that I can discuss this anymore right now. I apologize for any upset this causes you. I'll let you know when I'm ready to talk, and I appreciate your patience."

It's okay to be upset, to not know what to do, to be confused or hurt or angry—we can always speak from our heart. We can only move forward from where we are. Telling the truth, as always, liberates us.

About nine years ago, Francine and I were in Austin to see our family and attend the monthly Club meetings. We'd just had a nice lunch with a male friend of ours and were talking about a surgery I was scheduled to have soon. After I finished eating, I went back to our room to take a nap before the Club meeting that night. Francine and our friend Jack stayed at the restaurant to talk.

Francine and I agreed that she'd come back to our room at 5:30 PM so we could dress and get ready for the meeting. I took my nap and awoke promptly at 5:30, but Francine wasn't there yet. How well I remember the thoughts that popped into my head:

"Well, I guess Francine and Jack must be up in his hotel room, having wild sex and talking about what a lovely couple they'll make after I'm gone."

Two seconds later, I heard the key turn in the lock and Francine walked in. I didn't hesitate—I told her exactly what I had been thinking, and we laughed together at how silly I can be sometimes. The moral of the story? **Speak from your heart and trust that you are loved**.

Listening with compassion

If our partner is accusing and attacking or pushing us away and withdrawing, it can feel almost impossible to listen with compassion. But we must learn to look beyond their words and actions to what they are really trying to communicate and, ultimately, support them in asking for what they need.

Remember that when we listen with compassion, focusing on having a very deep appreciation of their experience, we give them the opportunity to see the truth for themselves. It can be challenging, but we all have the capacity to hear the pain behind the upset. Odds are, if your partner is that upset, they probably aren't fully aware of why they are hurting. We must strive to listen with compassion and give them the safety of our nonjudgmental love. We must put aside our need to defend, deflect, or explain and let them know that we are sorry they are upset.

**Remember—when we are heard, we are healed,
and the issues can then be dealt with
in partnership.**

Apologizing

As soon as we realize we've contributed to upsetting our partners, we must apologize. Remember the miraculous power of just being able to say, *"I'm sorry."* Apology disarms the emotional machinery that fuels upsets and enables us to get to the truth of what's driving it more quickly. When we apologize, we have a much better chance at dealing effectively with the situation in the moment, preventing resentments from building up unnecessarily. In the heat of an upset, apology can be our most valuable asset. I encourage people to apologize the moment any discord occurs between them and their partner—it couldn't hurt!

Try saying *"I'm sorry my upset scared you (or angered you) and I apologize for hurting you in any way"* or *"I'm sorry for whatever I said (or did) that may be upsetting you."* As we now know, apology is not an admission of guilt or wrong-doing—it's simply a loving way to let our partners know that we care about them and are willing to do what it takes to create safety. Once may not be enough—we might need to keep apologizing until our partner feels taken care of and harmony returns.

Forgiveness

Forgiveness is the fraternal twin of apology—they may not look exactly alike, but they come from the same mother.

Sometimes, if we feel wronged, it takes courage to accept our partner's apology. Since we are now aware of the price we pay for hauling around old injustices and grudges, we must forgive our partner for the mistakes he or she has made. **Remember this truth: they are human and they love you.** Forgiveness is a gift we give to each other and ourselves—when we let go of the need to punish or hold onto resentment, our partner has the chance to redeem themselves, to be whole again in our eyes. The result of forgiveness is a profound experience of restored trust and serenity.

When we're living in a state of forgiveness, many of the things our partner does won't irritate or upset us the way they used to. When we're trusting we are loved, we won't be as easily hurt, and the volume, intensity, and duration of upsets decreases dramatically. There will always be upsets in life; however, we will find that as we practice partnership and learn to communicate and listen, we won't spend nearly as much time slogging through the recycled upsets that used to follow us around.

We're all doing the best we can. We're all learning every day. Please forgive yourself and the people who love you.

Giving up the need to be self-righteous

One of our biggest challenges is to give up the need to be self-righteous about being right. We may believe we are right about whatever is going on, and that's fine. But when we use it as a weapon against our partner or lord it over them as a way of diminishing their feelings or point of view, then we are being **self-righteous**. We all know what it's like to be on the receiving end of that! No one likes to be bullied—and no matter how right we are, we can't shove it down our partner's throat and expect him or her to be grateful.

The problem with being attached to our self-righteousness is that it means the **other person must be wrong**—there's a break in the partnership that can be mended only by our letting go. This can be one of the hardest things for a human being to do, and yet the rewards are far greater than whatever petty satisfaction we may be feeling at that moment.

In any given upset, Francine and I will both have some valid points, but I used to always feel the need to have Francine agree with **my** point of view and admit that I was right before I'd be willing to forgive her. The temptation to hold onto being right was so strong. But what good does it do? No good. What purpose does it serve? No purpose, except to keep people apart. We may be right—but so what? Ultimately, the important thing is the well-being of the relationship.

Since our consummate goal is to create partnership, we must be willing to abandon the trap of self-righteousness. Try apologizing and saying, *"I'm sorry, but I'm feeling very self-righteous and judgmental right now. I know it hurts you, and I'm sorry. I know my need to be right provides nothing useful and causes you a lot of pain."* We must begin by noticing when we are stuck in being right and realize the cost of holding onto our position. We need to be willing to rise above pride and relinquish our attachment to being right for the sake of our partner.

Trusting we are loved

When we're listening we are loved, we hear what's actually being said. When we're not letting ourselves be loved, everything that's said or done becomes a potential upset:

- *"How could he do that if he really loved me?"*
- *"If she really loved me, she'd know that would upset me!"*

- *"He wouldn't stay at work so late if he really cared about me!"*
- *"She'd be more sensitive and not say that if she gave a damn about me!"*

On any given day in a relationship, there are countless opportunities to practice trusting we are loved. Remember my mantra—*"She loves me, she loves me"?* Trusting we are loved is both our deliverance from this kind of negative interpretation and the key to communicating and being heard.

We can't run away from our upsets

If we don't deal with our upsets, they may linger, sometimes gaining significance as the years go by. Ever bump into someone you haven't seen for years and still feel an uncomfortable strain between you? I'm sure it wouldn't take either of you longer than a few seconds to recall the upset that was never resolved. Until we practice forgiveness, we usually remember all the injustices done to us and carry them in our hearts.

When we are young, we want to leave home to get away from our parents and the problems we think they have caused us, but we end up taking ourselves along. We may feel that now we're immune, but the moment we think of our parents or speak to them on the telephone, the same old upsets are back. We can't wait to get off the phone, and we dread the holidays because we don't want to have to face those old, familiar situations.

It's draining and burdensome to resist the opportunity upsets provide. We all must ask ourselves what we can do to handle our upsets in a way that facilitates healing and growth. We may also need to look at some of the ancient hurts and lingering resentments that haunt us and take some action toward bringing them to completion. In some instances, forgiveness might be all that it takes. For other situations, communication is the way through.

The opportunity of upsets

As someone who has spent a lot of his life being upset, I can tell you that learning how to handle upsets responsibly has had a remarkable effect on the health of my relationships. I have always been quick to jump to conclusions, but I have accepted this about myself. I've become much better at recovering quickly, and it usually takes me only a few seconds or minutes to realize what is really happening underneath my annoyance or anger.

We all have the power to nurture ourselves and the people we love in the way we deal with upsets. Each time we go beyond the way we've reacted automatically in the past and stay focused on our commitment to discovering the opportunity inherent in the upset, we strengthen and enhance our relationships immeasurably.

We don't need to live in fear of upsets anymore. They are not an indication that anything is wrong, only that we are engaged in being alive. When we realize that we can deal with our upsets in healthier ways, we no longer avoid or invalidate them. **Upsets happen!**

Remember: **The measure of a healthy relationship is not necessarily whether or not upsets occur, but how quickly we can recover from them, enhanced and enriched by their healing lessons.** When we live in the embrace of partnership, upsets are transformed into yet another portal towards growth and unity with our loved ones.

CHAPTER 9

Expressing Appreciation

The greatest gift we can give humankind is to
love and let ourselves be loved.

We need to be appreciated

When I think of appreciation and what it means to us, I recall the saying: "When someone's on their deathbed, their last words never are *'I wish I'd spent more time at the office.'*" As we get older and people come and go in our lives, one of our most common regrets is: "*I wish I'd told her how I felt.... I wish I'd said 'I love you' to him.... I took her for granted.... Why couldn't I have appreciated him more when we were together?*"

I'm sure all of us can think of at least a few instances when we really cared for someone but didn't tell them. Now they're gone—either out of our lives or passed away, and we're left with the realization that they may never know how much they meant to us. Of course we need to forgive ourselves, but we also need to become more aware of how important it is to appreciate those we love, admire, and respect—**right now**.

When I've asked people who are unhappy in their jobs what they feel is lacking, the response I hear most frequently is: *"I don't feel appreciated."* When I ask people who are unhappy in their relationships the same question, I often hear: *"I feel taken for granted. I just don't feel appreciated."*

From the moment we became conscious and took human form, we've had a need to be appreciated—noticed for our uniqueness, honored for our efforts, acknowledged for just being who we are. When I think of how basic this need is, I recall the press coverage a few years back about the Romanian orphanages that had sprung up all over their country in the wake of political upheaval to deal with the deluge of infants and young children left homeless.

There was a lot of controversy surrounding these orphanages. The world saw disturbing images of babies left in their cribs for days without human touch—only the briefest contact was made when they were diapered or handed a bottle. These children were not held, played with, or even lovingly spoken to—only the most generic care was given for their physical survival—and most of them were extremely damaged emotionally. They stared at the video cameras, their little haunted eyes gazing out of hollow faces, babies looking like old men and women. Others rocked themselves hypnotically in their cribs, back and forth, side to side, desperately trying to give themselves comfort. Still others banged their heads on their cribs or even on the walls—wailing and crying out to be loved.

These videotapes and photographs broke the hearts of the whole world, and many groups of people came forward wanting to adopt these children. These good-hearted parents hoped to give the babies what they had been deprived of for too long. I remember reading about some of the cases and how difficult it was for many of these children to accept the love and affection that their adoptive parents offered. They had developed what is called Attachment Disorder—a syndrome that occurs when human beings are not touched, stroked, sung to, held, or otherwise nurtured in infancy. They had lost their ability to "attach" themselves to another human being—to show affection or receive it. Some of the children slowly recovered in the patient glow of their parent's commitment—sadly, some were so wounded that they didn't make any progress at all. It was such a tragic situation—all these parents wanted was to give these babies what they desperately needed—but the long-standing deprivation had atrophied the ability of these children to trust they could be loved.

I tell this story to illustrate how fundamental it is to need, to actually crave appreciation. As we all know, food, clothing, and shelter are only one small part of the equation when it comes to truly nourishing a living being. One has only to look at dogs kept a long time in cages at the animal shelter to see that getting enough to eat and a having a place to sleep is only the beginning of health and well-being. The dogs remind us of the forgotten children—they stare passively, eyes empty. They've long since stopped wagging their tails and trying to get someone to pay attention to them. They've given up.

The bottom line is: we need to know **we matter**. We need to live in the experience that we are known, honored, noticed, important, valued, and cherished.

What do people really want most from other people? Is it money, position, power? If it were money, then who would volunteer at their local school or hospital? Would people join the Peace Corps or work all night on a 24-hour suicide hotline? If it were power, then all dictators would be happy people. But that's not what we truly want from one another. We want to be appreciated, respected, acknowledged—it's often more important than money or power, prestige or fame. Recently, while watching a motion picture awards show, I observed these well-known actors basking in the adoration of their peers and realized yet again that for them it means more than any critic's review or box-office receipt. However, we need to be applauded not only for accomplishments or efforts, but also for our very presence in each others' lives. Sadly, many people feel this essential experience is lacking in both their jobs and relationships. We must learn how to fully express our appreciation for one another.

Appreciate means: 1) *To recognize the quality, significance, or magnitude of;* 2) *To be fully aware of or sensitive to;* 3) *To be thankful or show gratitude for,* and 4) *To admire greatly; value.*

Acknowledgment is the partner of appreciation. In Part Two, Chapter Three, I gave the definition of acknowledgment simply as: *To admit the existence, reality, or truth of.* However, in this case, I also include the second part of that definition: *To recognize as being valid or having force or power,* and *to express thanks or gratitude for.*

The experience of being appreciated is often the result of being acknowledged. Since appreciation and acknowledgment go hand-in-hand, I will use both terms interchangeably in this chapter.

The importance of speaking our appreciation

How often do we find ourselves in the presence of another human being and have the thought, *"She's a good listener. I feel great every time I talk to her. What a kind, thoughtful person."*

We have the thought, but we often don't speak it. Why? Sometimes it's because we don't want to appear foolish, or we're afraid we'll embarrass her. But most of the time it's because we don't think our comments would really matter or make a difference. We may say to ourselves:

"She has to know how terrific she is. People probably tell her all the time."

One thing I'm certain of is that people often **don't** know how terrific they are! People **need** to hear what we think of them! We assume that people know how much we appreciate them—after all, we **do**, so they must realize it. What a missed opportunity! Here we are thinking we're not appreciated enough when, in fact, we are—but no one bothers to say anything!

I believe that since many of us feel so taken for granted in our lives, we don't give much thought to appreciating others. It's human nature—when we feel loved, we want to share it with the world. When we feel unloved, we tend to shrink back inside ourselves and get stingy about it. The act of speaking our appreciation, like compassion, must sometimes be consciously generated— created purposefully.

When we acknowledge people, we help turn down the volume of the *"I'm not important, valued, and loved"* voice-over. Since we all hear that voice in varying degrees of loudness, we can make a qualitative difference in someone's experience of themselves when we openly express our gratefulness and praise. **If we hold back our true feelings, we'll never know the contribution we could have made if we had just said something!**

Honoring the people we love

When we thank someone, we strengthen them. When a parent tells a child, *"It feels so good knowing that I can trust you to do your homework without nagging,"* we are doing much more than validating them—we are, in fact, **helping to create their own experience of themselves**. When we say to our partner, *"Thank you for loving me,"* we are giving them a powerful message: *"Not only do I love you, but I also know you love me."* Remember, when we forget we are loved, we are in pain. Saying *"Thank you for loving me"* **creates** trusting we are loved. When your partner comes home tonight, greet him or her at the door and say, *"Thank you for loving me!"*

On the other hand, we dishonor others when we put our own limitations and restrictions on them. For instance, how many of us live inside the boxes others put us in? If someone thinks we're "pushy" they will see us through the confines of that thought. When we decide someone is a certain way, every interaction we have with them only serves to solidify our perception. For instance, if we view our partner as "overly sensitive" or "emotional," that's how they'll show up—it's guaranteed! It's totally valid for them to be upset, but we'll think they're overreacting because, after all, they're so "emotional." Our self-righteousness makes it virtually impossible to see who they really are and give them the compassion they deserve.

We may have something to do with their upset, but we can't own up to our part in it because *"they're overly sensitive and get hurt by the simplest little thing."* This is a way we avoid having to take responsibility for the impact our judgments have on our partner. These lenses we see one another through keep us and our loved ones disabled—it's hard to expand when we're trapped in such a tiny box.

We all categorize people—it's a form of judgment. However, in the interests of partnership, we must be willing to see how we have dishonored others with the labels we may have pasted on their foreheads. It takes courage to admit that we have held each other back with our judgments—and even more courage to give these judgments up.

We stifle ourselves and others when we impose limits on them. It's time to tap back into our fullest appreciation of the people in our lives—to honor and value them for the extraordinary beings they are. Here is a Reader's Digest condensation of an article written by Patricia McGeer. It was given to me many years ago and has become one of my favorite stories:

When I sailed to Kiniwata, an island in the Pacific, I took along a notebook. After I got back, it was filled with descriptions of flora and fauna, native customs and costumes. But the only note that still interests me is the one that says, "Johnny Lingo gave eight cows to Sarita's father." I'm reminded of this story every time I see a woman belittling her husband or a wife withering under her husband's scorn. I want to say to them, "You should know why Johnny Lingo paid eight cows for his wife."

Johnny Lingo wasn't exactly his name, but that's what Shenkin, the manager of the guest house, called him. Johnny was mentioned by many people in many connec-

tions. If I wanted to spend a few days on the neighboring island of Nurabandi, Johnny Lingo could put me up. If I wanted to fish, he could show me where the biting was best. If it was pearls I sought, he would bring me the best buys. The people of Kiniwata all spoke highly of Johnny Lingo. Yet when they spoke, they smiled and the smiles were slightly mocking.

"Get Johnny Lingo to help you find what you want and let him do the bargaining," advised Shenkin. "Johnny knows how to make a deal."

"Johnny Lingo!" a boy seated nearby hooted the name and rocked with laughter.

"What goes on?" I demanded. "Everybody tells me to get in touch with Johnny Lingo and then starts laughing. Let me in on the joke."

"Oh, the people like to laugh," Shenkin said, shrugging. "Johnny's the brightest, the strongest young man in the islands. And for his age, the richest."

"But if he's all you say, what is there to laugh about?"

"Only one thing. Five months ago, at fall festival, Johnny came to Kiniwata and found himself a wife. He paid her father eight cows."

I knew enough about island customs to be impressed. Two or three cows could buy a fair-to-middling wife, four or five cows, a highly satisfactory one.

"Good Lord!" I said. "Eight cows! She must have beauty that takes your breath away."

"She's not ugly," he conceded and smiled a little. "But the kindest could only call Sarita plain. Sam Karoo, her father, was afraid she'd be left on his hands."

"But then he got eight cows for her? Is that extraordinary?"

"Never been paid before."

"Yet you call Johnny's wife plain?"

"I said it would be kindness to call her plain. She was skinny. She walked with her shoulders hunched and her head ducked. She was scared of her own shadow."

"Well," I said, "I guess there's just no accounting for love."

"True enough," agreed the man. "And that's why the villagers grin when they talk about Johnny. They get special satisfaction from the fact that the sharpest trader in the islands was bested by dull old Sam Karoo."

"But how?"

"No one knows and everyone wonders. All the cousins were urging Sam to wait until Johnny offered to pay one cow—then they wanted him to ask for three cows and hold out for two. Then Johnny came to Sam Karoo and said, 'Father of Sarita, I offer eight cows for your daughter.'"

"Eight cows," I murmured. "I'd like to meet this Johnny Lingo."

I wanted fish. I wanted pearls. So the next afternoon I beached my boat at Nurabandi. And I noticed as I asked *directions to Johnny's house that his name brought no sly smile to the lips of his fellow Nurabandians. And when I met the slim, serious young man, when he welcomed me with grace to his home, I was glad that from his own people he had respect unmingled with mockery.*

We sat in his house and talked. Then he asked, "You come here from Kiniwata?"

"Yes."

"They speak of me on that island?"

"They say there's nothing I might want that you can't help me get."

He smiled gently. "My wife is from Kiniwata."

"Yes, I know."

"They speak of her?"

"A little."

"What do they say?"

"Why, just . . ." The question caught me off balance. "They told me you were married at festival time."

"Nothing more?" The curve of his eyebrows told me he knew there had to be more.

"They also say the marriage settlement was eight cows." I paused. "They wonder why."

"They ask that?" His eyes lighted with pleasure. *"Everyone in Kiniwata knows about the eight cows?"*

I nodded.

"And in Nurabandi everyone knows it too." His chest expanded with satisfaction. *"Always and forever, when they speak of marriage settlements, it will be remembered that Johnny Lingo paid eight cows for Sarita."*

So that's the answer, I thought. Vanity.

And then I saw her. I watched her enter the room to place flowers on the table. She stood still a moment to smile at the young man beside me. Then she went swiftly out again. She was the most beautiful woman I have ever seen. The lift of her shoulders, the lilt of her chin, the sparkle of her eyes all spelled a pride to which no one could deny her the right.

I turned back to Johnny Lingo and found him looking at me.

"You admire her," he murmured.

"She . . . she's glorious. But she's not Sarita from Kiniwata," I said.

"There's only one Sarita. Perhaps she doesn't look the way they say she looked in Kiniwata."

"She doesn't. I heard she was homely. They all make fun of you because you let yourself be cheated by Sam Karoo."

"You think eight cows were too many?" A smile slid over his lips.

"No. But how can she be so different?"

"Do you ever think," he asked, "what it must mean to a woman to know that her husband has settled on the lowest price for which she can be bought? And then later, when the women talk, they boast of what their husbands paid for them. One says four cows, another maybe six. This could not happen to my Sarita."

"Then you did this just to make your wife happy?"

"I wanted Sarita to be happy, yes. But I wanted more than that. You say she is different. This is true. Many things can change a woman. Things that happen inside, things that happen outside. But the thing that matters most is what she thinks about herself. In Kiniwata, Sarita believed she was worth nothing. Now she knows she is worth more than any other woman in the islands."

"Then you wanted—"

"I wanted to marry Sarita. I loved her and no other woman."

"But"—I was close to understanding.

"But," he finished softly, "I wanted an eight-cow wife."

Remember the musical "My Fair Lady"? When Eliza Doolittle was treated like a lady, she became one. She rose to the occasion in the eyes of those who saw her beauty and innate worth. What transformed her from a lowly flower girl into an elegant, sophisticated young woman? **It was in how she was regarded**—and it took Henry Higgins quite a while to see how he was hurting her with his insensitive reminders of "who she really was." Everyone is magnificent when we appreciate them fully. We are all "eight-cow" wives and husbands—let's create an environment in our homes that promotes, not hinders the growth of our partner. Magic happens when we honor the ones we love.

The challenge of receiving appreciation

If feeling appreciated is so important, why aren't we magnets for it? We want it but we're often uncomfortable accepting it. We deflect or don't take it seriously—thinking that our partner and loved ones *"don't really mean it."* Why do we do that? Because **we don't trust that we are loved and don't trust the people who express their love for us.** We put up walls when appreciation comes our way because most of us are still working on believing that we deserve to be acknowledged. Some have a hard time accepting even the most minor of compliments.

- *"Oh, I love that dress!"*

  "This thing? Yeah, I got it on sale—quite a bargain. I wish I could afford nicer things, though."

- *"Your new haircut looks great!"*

  "You really think so? I hate it—I thought I wanted it this short but now I think I've made a big mistake."

- *"You did a real nice job on that presentation."*

  "Oh, it wasn't such a big deal—anybody could have put that stuff together—I was just the one who had the time."

- *"Your house looks fantastic!"*

   "You must be joking—it's a mess!"

In light of the examples above, I would like to propose another, however revolutionary, response to all of the above statements: Say *"Thank you."*

When we are acknowledged, we often appraise it first—looking to see if we agree with it or not. If we do, we're more likely to accept it. If we don't, we reject it (and sometimes the person giving it!). We assess the acknowledgment through our standards about whether or not we "deserve" it. If we feel we do, only then will we allow ourselves to accept it.

However, when we deflect acknowledgment, we are in essence saying, *"What you just said is not the truth—you don't know the half of it."* We invalidate the experience of the other person but aren't even aware of it because we're being so hard on ourselves. Why is it so hard to just say *"Thank you"?* We all know what it feels like to be on the receiving end of someone who won't accept our acknowledgment—it can be very upsetting when we want to give our love or appreciation and it's rejected.

The other thing going on underneath those self-deprecating remarks we make is false modesty, a lesson we've been taught by well-meaning parents who didn't want us to appear conceited or arrogant. *"Don't blow your own horn,"* we were told. But we actually do great harm to ourselves and others when we deny the truth of their experience of us.

Conversely, we do a great service when we let ourselves be appreciated. There's something life-affirming about being able to graciously accept a compliment—not only does it strengthen our own self-esteem, it empowers the other person as well. We all want to have a positive influence on others. When we say how great someone looks and they respond with *"No, you're wrong—I don't,"* it can knock the wind out of our sails. We offered ourselves and our offering was snubbed. On the other hand, when our compliments are greeted as suggested below, we'll feel just as good as they do—maybe better!

- *"Your new haircut looks great!"*

  "Thanks! I was feeling a little down, but you've made my day!"

- *"You did a real nice job on that presentation."*

  "Thanks a lot. I really worked hard on it— it's gratifying to know people notice."

These small examples of appreciation may seem insignificant, but I believe that no expression of love is ever insignificant. Sometimes one gentle word or generous comment from someone—said at precisely the right time—can help put us back on the right road. And we can return the favor by doing the same act of kindness for the people in our life.

We contribute to others when we allow them to contribute to us.

When someone honors us with a compliment, even if we don't agree it's warranted, we owe it to them to accept it—for our sake and theirs. Honor the ones who care for you—who have the willingness to take the time to notice something they like and express it.

And do you know what's really marvelous? **It really isn't for us to judge whether or not we are worthy of someone's admiration**. The majesty of letting ourselves be loved is that whatever is said to us is the experience of

that other person, and it is **the truth** for them! Even
better, their experience may often be more valid than our
own (and perhaps overly-critical) view of ourselves.
Thank God there are other people who can see more than
we can see! That's the good news! We're all harder on
ourselves than we are on others—so let's honor another's
experience and perhaps learn something about who we
really are.

I often told my children as they were growing up,
*"People don't think about you the way you think about you.
People are too busy thinking about themselves."* It's true, most
of us have impossibly high standards for ourselves that
we would never demand from others. We all have a
tendency to look beyond each other's imperfections to
see the true beauty within. Instead of rejecting people's
observations, we might want to be thankful that they see
our magnificence even when we can't! When we allow
love to infiltrate our barricades and fortresses, we find
out that there's really no need to protect ourselves—we
are safe.

**This is one of the most valuable aspects of appre-
ciation—through the eyes of another we might see
ourselves more accurately—and more compassion-
ately.** To invalidate their experience robs both us and
them of the joy of loving and letting ourselves be loved.

Thank you for saying that

Many years ago when the Clubs began, I found myself
starting to make a statement: *"Thank you for saying that."*
After someone would share a feeling or observation, it
seemed like the most natural thing in the world to thank
them for having the courage or awareness to bring their

thoughts to the group. It wasn't necessarily a statement of agreement or approval—it was an acknowledgment.

When someone has the courage to state their feelings or contribute an insight, I like to acknowledge it with a simple *"Thank you for saying that."* It feels good to say and good to hear. I believe that thanking people is an essential part of the healing process. We can give thanks as a way of expressing appreciation for the contributions people make to us every day.

- *"Thanks for having compassion for me."*
- *"Thank you for apologizing."*
- *"Thank you for being in my life."*
- *"Thank you for loving me."*
- *"Thanks for being my friend."*
- *"Thank you for all that you do to make our lives better."*
- *"Thank you for forgiving me."*
- *"Thank you for listening."*
- *"Thank you for trusting me."*
- *"Thanks for letting me love you."*

Notice what's working

To master the art of appreciation, we must learn to look at our partners differently. Because we are naturally judgmental and often view life with a critical eye, it's so much easier to notice **what we don't like** about the circumstances—i.e., **what's not working**. Although becoming clear about what's not working is a necessary step in our process of improving a situation, human beings have a tendency to zero in on what we think is wrong and **stay there**. To create partnership, we must learn to strike a balance between the two and find new ways to effect change through positive reinforcement, not solely through criticism.

The act of noticing what's working is analogous to physical health—when our bodies are functioning well, we don't have much attention on them. We don't often consciously feel grateful for all the work our stomach has to do to prepare our food for its trip into our intestines, or take a moment each day to say thank you to our liver for detoxifying and cleansing our blood. But when we feel nauseated or get a sharp pain in our abdomen, our awareness is suddenly targeted to these organs and we may begin to worry about them, or at the very least be reminded of their existence.

In dealing with others, we do much the same thing. When life is just humming along, we may not even notice why it's working. But the moment we don't feel heard or we think we've been wronged, suddenly we sit up and take notice! And not only do we notice, but we're also likely to feel the need to let our partner know in no uncertain terms how upset we are with what they've done. This condition exists in most relationships—and it usually leads to people feeling that they are not appreciated and can't do anything well enough to please their partner. We feel we can't win—it seems as though our positive qualities are taken for granted, and our slip-ups are being documented with alarming precision.

We've all seen this occur in our relationships, and it makes sense. If all we do is complain and point out the faults and weaknesses of our partner, how can we expect him or her to feel good about themselves and us? Perhaps you are frequently on the receiving end of this kind of unconscious nit-picking. How does it feel? Wouldn't you like your partner to be as conscious of all that's successful about you with the same accuracy that he or she calls attention to your flaws?

For us to begin appreciating all the kind, noble, and generous acts our partner does every day, attention must be paid. We need to look upon these people with whom we share our lives with respect, admiration, and grateful hearts. **It's time to make a commitment to start sharing our acknowledgment as freely as we used to share our complaints.** See the miracle that occurs when our partner and other loved ones actually experience being appreciated. We can do so much for one another when we come from love! Our kindness has divine power.

Can anyone be shamed or browbeaten into becoming attentive, responsible, generous? Never. We need to own up to the fact that we have a part to play in our partner's well-being—our negative views and belittling of them have been hurtful. It's time to realize that we can only help each other heal when we give up the need to criticize. Appreciation moves bigger mountains than blame ever could, and gentleness is the only true power in the world.

I'm reminded of one of Aesop's fables—the Sun and the Wind were having an argument over who was the most powerful:

The Wind said he was, since he could knock over tall trees and set the sea to flooding. He said that his force could topple huge boulders and carve holes in stone, shape deserts and send giant storms all over the world. How could the Sun ever compete with that kind of power?

The Sun only nodded, and observed a man walking on the road below. "Well, Wind," said he, "let's put our strengths to the test. See that man down there? I'll make you a wager that I can make him take off his coat before you can."

"Ha!" said the haughty Wind. "That's no contest! I'll send my coldest, iciest wind down on him and his coat will fly off in a second!" And with that, the Wind did as he had promised, and the man's coat began to flap about in the frigid breeze. But instead of his coat blowing off, the man gripped it tighter, pulling it closer and closer to his shivering body. He stood still, his arms locked solidly in front of him, braving the cold. The Wind, frustrated and angry, blew even harder. But the more he sent the raging force of his freezing blast down upon the poor man, the tighter the man held his coat.

Finally the Sun could no longer endure the man's suffering and began to shine his tender, loving rays. The warmth pierced through the icy gale and slowly filtered down. Gratefully, the man looked up. The Wind watched in dismay as the Sun's rays shone hotter and hotter. The man lifted his face to the sky, basking in the relief from the awful chill.

After only a few minutes, the Sun's heat became so great that the man began to sweat and opened his coat. The man took a handkerchief from his pocket to wipe his brow, and then, to the Wind's horror, peeled the coat from his shoulders. He folded it over his arm and continued his walk, whistling as he went.

The Sun only smiled gently at his proud friend the Wind and said, "Kindness has power when strength and force often fail."

If we demand that our partners change, improve, or get better, we are probably acting like the Wind. If we genuinely want them to grow and heal, we need to start behaving like the Sun.

Being appreciated means letting yourself be loved

When we don't trust that we are loved, it can be a struggle to accept that people know and appreciate us—it's also difficult to believe that our acknowledgment of another would matter. When we don't trust that we are loved, we hold back from expressing appreciation and allowing others to do the same. At the deepest level, our quality of life is determined by our ability to deal with the disappointments, unexpected upsets, and misunderstandings inherent in day-to-day living, and this ability is enhanced by **remembering that we are loved**.

Remembering this can be one of our most compelling goals, one that is renewed and recreated in each moment. When I forget that I am loved, I am in pain. My life's work is to recover and remind myself of the truth—**I am loved**. Simple, but not easy.

We are so blessed, you and I. However, there will always be things we don't have or think we want, always be something else out there that looks better than what we have right here. That's human nature. **We must remember that where we are is exactly where we need to be and that whatever is going on in our world is exactly what needs to happen to serve our highest good.** I believe that all the suffering we experience has at its source the lack of trust in the process of life, and can be traced back to one or more of the following states:

1. **Regretting the past**
2. **Invalidating the present**
3. **Fearing the future**

Much has been said and written about living in the present, appreciating what we have and counting our blessings. We have lived with that awareness, yet we still struggle with being able to fully appreciate the abundance around us. As we strive and grow, let us remember that we are safe in the embrace of God—we always have been, and always will be.

Seeking out the best in others and encouraging them is truly God's work. Let's stop holding back and honor our dearest ones with the knowledge that they mean the world to us. Let us all make a commitment to consciously express our gratitude for what they do, who they are, and where they are headed, as we heal together in this most amazing experience of being profoundly known, appreciated, and loved.

CHAPTER 10

Honoring Your Commitment

When we think, "I don't want to commit until I'm
sure it will work out," we've got it backwards.

What is commitment?

I heard a rather sobering, unfunny joke recently: Some women now look at potential husbands and wonder, *"Is this the kind of man I want my children to spend every other weekend with?"* We're so afraid that our relationships won't work out or last—and many of them don't—so commitment starts to look obsolete. We either misunderstand it—we may think it's a trap or a prison sentence—or we have become cynical, believing it doesn't mean anything anymore.

Yet, despite our considerations, **we want commitment**—we want the certainty that comes from feeling safe inside its protective embrace. But we're also afraid—afraid that if we want it, the other person won't, or if we insist on having it, the other person will turn tail and run. This kind of thinking can lead to the **I will if you will syndrome**—like children on a dare. We don't want to commit until we know there's a **guarantee**—we'll wait and test the waters, see how it feels, but won't take the plunge **until we're sure**. Putting our toe in the pool without jumping in is like waiting until we learn how to swim before going in the water.

- *"I'll wait until he proves he loves me."*
- *"What if I fall out of love with her?"*
- *"What if I'm making a mistake?"*
- *"What if the problems we're having get worse?"*
- *"What if she finds someone she loves even more?"*

Avoiding commitment is like buying something on speculation—give it a test run and see how it drives before we lay down the cash. This approach may work with a car, but it's deadly to a relationship. Why?

Because it creates a situation in which people don't feel safe—without commitment, we're always worried that sooner or later everything will fall apart. It's like a huge boulder precariously balanced on a precipice—it hasn't fallen yet, but it's inevitable. In five minutes or five years from now, a strong wind or a hard rain will push it over the edge. Who wants to live with that kind of anxiety? And yet we do—and wonder why the relationship founders.

The power of commitment, whether we are embarking on a project, a mountain climb, or a relationship, is in the stand that we take:

**I will honor my commitment
regardless of the circumstances,
whether I feel I want to or not,
without hesitation.**

This is a pledge that we give and then honor with
every fiber of our being. All the beauty and majesty that
we are comes forth from that declaration. All the great
works in this world were realized by people who had a
vision, confronted the obstacles, and triumphed.

It takes a special courage and willingness to devote
ourselves to making a partnership work. The ability to
make a choice and see it through is one of the noblest
expressions of being human. Imagine being in a relationship where you and your partner declared your
unconditional commitment to work out your issues
together forever, no matter what.

When we know that we and our partner are in it for
the long haul, we become safe inside that structure, and
in safety, we can deal with **anything**. Instead of seeing
conflicts or upsets as evidence that it's not working, we
live in a framework called commitment—and in that
loving environment, whatever comes up is just the
next thing to deal with, not something to be resisted
or feared.

Why make a commitment?

Commitment makes a path through the forest—there
may be brambles and boulders and bears, but if we stay
on the path, we're okay. Commitment gives us a sense of
purpose and a context for our actions, behavior, and
thoughts. When we feel wounded in our relationship
with a loved one, we might want to run away, leave, hurt

them, get even, show them we don't care. But when we are committed, these feelings are just feelings, not prime directives—we don't use them to create a case for ending the relationship. Living inside a commitment doesn't mean we don't have doubts, anger, or fears—it means we don't give them any more significance than they deserve.

When we make a commitment, we dedicate ourselves to creating a solid foundation that we and our partner can count on. We trust ourselves and we are trusted. There is less uncertainty—we don't stand in the woods very long, wondering what to do. We know which path to get on as soon as we get sidetracked.

What happens when we aren't committed?

When we aren't committed, **each conflict calls the relationship into question**. We're in a constant state of anxiety—wondering if this upset will be the one that makes us or our partner leave. There's always the option to bail out, so the relationship is constantly in jeopardy. Who can live with that kind of stress?—and yet many of us do it every day, because we haven't jumped in the pool. We're still wandering around the perimeter, looking at the water and trying to figure out how to swim without getting wet. So we open ourselves up to mental mischief, all variations on the same theme:

- *"Can we work through this? How can I know for sure?"*
- *"Is this the right person? If so, would we be having all these problems?"*
- *"Should I stay (or leave)?"*
- *"Will I regret it (if I stay or leave)?"*

This kind of questioning takes a lot of energy and drains our ability to deal with what's actually happening. In the absence of commitment, both people feel insecure, which makes it almost impossible to move forward. When we are committed, our energy goes toward resolving problems because doing so is all in a day's work in relationship. When we are not committed, upsets only serve as wedges to drive us further apart.

I'm completely committed to my relationship with Francine. In this one woman, I've found all women, and my inner conversation about *"How long will this one last?"* ended ages ago. We've grown up together and learned how to take care of each other. Both of us are committed to create an environment of safety and forgiveness; and from that place, we've each become far more than we could have become on our own. **That's the miracle of commitment.**

What are we waiting for?

When Francine and I first got together, we decided not to get married—we'd live together but not sign the paper. One day I asked Francine to remind me why we weren't getting married. She said,

"Well, since we've both been married before, and aren't going to have more children, why bother with the legal hassle in case in five years or so it doesn't work out?"

Amazingly, even as she said the words, she realized that this philosophy was totally inconsistent with the unconditional commitment we had made to each other and the relationship. This conversation turned the key— it showed us we were living in the philosophy of **"I've got one foot out the door—just in case!"** Our wedding was held six weeks later, and we've been married for twenty-five years.

Francine knows she can count on me to make our partnership my priority. She's not intimidated by my ups and downs. In my presence, in my home, and in my life, she is honored, loved, and safe. As you've noticed from the stories I've shared about our lives together, we have all kinds of arguments and upsets. But it's my commitment I ultimately honor, not my automatic responses—allowing me to get back in the saddle, ready to do whatever it takes to recover and move forward.

The challenge of commitment

Sometimes, even after we move in with our loved one or get married, we're still asking ourselves the question:

"Did I make a mistake?"

I don't believe that there is any couple, even the ones who seem to be so in love and well-suited for each other, who have not had similar thoughts right before or after the wedding! We notice some new character flaw in our prospective partner, or we realize that the thing we wish would have changed about them hasn't—and wonder if it ever will. It is normal and human to have these thoughts, but we give them undue weight and meaning. We are afraid to say them to our partner because they might be thinking the same thing!

But who are we really asking when we wonder, *"Will this last?"* What are we waiting for—a message from on high, fate, a quiz in a magazine, or our partner to reveal the answer?

The mysterious "it"

"I wonder if it's going to work?"

What is "it"? And why do we give "it" so much power?

Well, "it" isn't anything other than what we make "it." When we think in terms of "it," then "it" becomes somehow outside ourselves and we relinquish responsibility. There's no magic formula for making "it" work—the truth is, "it" works when we **say** "it" will work!

Whatever we call our union—a relationship, marriage, commitment, partnership, whatever—those terms are only guidelines which provide us with the opportunity to create partnership. A relationship is not a fire by which we passively warm our hands—it needs constant replenishing by both people. While we wait for our partner to stoke the fire and fan the flames, we may watch our love flicker and die. If we are to stay warm through the coming cold winters, both people need to take full responsibility for the relationship.

When we make a commitment, we have taken personal responsibility to make it work. We have some choice here—we're not just going along for the ride. Commitment becomes the keystone—without it, whatever we build will have a substandard foundation and could easily collapse. There are many challenges ahead, and commitment is the mortar that solidifies our vows.

And speaking of vows, how I wish it could all just be handled by the ones we speak on our wedding day! It would be nice if all we had to do was say the words once and that would be all there was to it. Unfortunately, that's sometimes where the trouble begins. We speak the ultimate commitment before God, but don't fully realize what we're signing on for.

Some of us are still hoping the other person will "make us happy," or that getting married will instantly solve all our problems. We often aren't aware that we've entered into marriage with a mental picture of what relationship is supposed to look like, and how that picture prevents us from **being fully in the marriage we really have**. When we marry, we are coming out of the gate with the most challenging times still to come—the real relationship is just beginning.

Half the marriages in this country end in divorce. Speaking our commitment at our wedding is **our initial promise**—it is not the be-all and the end-all. It's like our partner asking, *"Why do I need to say 'I love you' over and over? I told you on our wedding night, isn't that enough?"* Well, obviously it isn't, and the same holds true with commitment. We don't commit ourselves to something and then just forget about it—when the obstacles come up, we have to recommit over and over again. We have to breathe life into it—saying the words once isn't enough.

Our commitment has to be cultivated, demonstrated, strengthened over time. But many of us, even though we give our pledge, don't fully understand what we're promising. We think we're saying, *"for better or worse"* but inside we're saying *"...until it doesn't feel good anymore or gets too uncomfortable."* We think we're committed but we're not—instead of seeing conflict as normal and an opportunity to heal, we decide this person isn't the right one, and we divorce.

I'm not suggesting that there is never an appropriate time to divorce—sometimes it's the only way. But I have met hundreds of people who, if they could have obtained the tools and support they needed in times of crisis, would never have ended their relationship. When we don't take the opportunities that arise and dissolve the partnership, we usually bring the unresolved issues with us into the next relationship. The new person may initially appear to be very different, but as time goes by, they somehow begin to seem more and more like our former spouse. It's nature's way—we are in relationship to be healed, and if we don't do the work with our present partner, we may have to start all over again with someone else.

However, sometimes one or both people get to a place where it becomes clear that the relationship, in its present form, has become detrimental to the health and growth of the individuals involved.

Commitment to partnership

And what happens if circumstances arise that make it inappropriate or impossible for two people to stay in a marriage or other exclusive arrangement? It is here that our **commitment to partnership in relationship** can provide a bridge, supporting us even when our relationships change. When we declare our commitment to loving and honoring another human being, our declaration can extend **even beyond the form the relationship takes**.

Living in the spirit of partnership means that whatever occurs, both people are committed to taking care of one another's well-being, even if it becomes necessary to end the relationship or alter it drastically. Being committed to partnership, no matter what the circumstances of the relationship, is particularly useful when there are children involved. Staying in partnership is extremely important when we are co-parenting, especially when a marriage is in the process of dissolving. Ultimately, the best way we can take care of our children is to remain in partnership.

When we are committed to being in partnership, we are empowered to continue the healing process. In the embrace of partnership, our commitment to the well-being of the other person and the well-being of the relationship **is still the priority**.

Commitment casts out fear

When we are committed, our fear cannot rule us—the thoughts we have don't stand a chance. We have no control over our initial thoughts, but we **do** have a choice about which ones we believe are **the truth**. We can learn to recognize them for what they are—just little birds passing overhead. There goes one. There goes another one! Just let them fly by. They don't have any inherent meaning other than what we give them. **Thoughts aren't real unless we make them real**. It's another one of those spiritual muscles we have to work over time, noticing when we are giving our thoughts too much power. We can strengthen our ability to **have** our thoughts instead of **letting them have us**.

You might have the thought, *"I want to leave him,"* but you don't have to do it. When we are committed, the thoughts don't take root and grow into huge oak trees—they just shrivel and blow away. Wouldn't it be freeing to know that no matter how angry or afraid we became, we wouldn't be abandoned? What a comfort to just have our thoughts and feelings without fearing sooner or later that our partner will get fed up and say, *"Okay, I've had it! That's the last straw!"* and walk out on us forever.

How commitment affects conflict

As mentioned earlier, one of the most persistent misconceptions about relationships is that once we find the right person, we won't have upsets—at least not any significant ones. Ask any happily married person—it's not so! **The truth is, *not* being committed causes *more* upsets, because when people feel like they're on probation, they are more prone to insecurity and doubting that they are loved—which leads to more upsets**! When we are committed, we still get upset, but we no longer need to justify or withhold our true feelings or threaten to leave.

In the context of our commitment, everything that happens is okay—it's **included** in the relationship. We don't blow it out of proportion. When we're not expending energy on trying to keep our relationships from falling apart, we can then pay attention to enhancing them.

Why do men seem more afraid of commitment?

Commitment seems easier for women most of the time; however, the idea of commitment strikes fear in the hearts of many men—even though I'm certain that's what they really want. To some men, commitment translates into something like a jail term. Even the language used sounds like a prison sentence:

- *"I'll be **trapped**! She'll get her **hooks in me** for good."*
- *"You mean **give up** all other women forever? That's cruel and unusual **punishment**!"*
- *"I refuse to be **tied down**. I'm not ready for that."*
- *"She's always **pressuring** me to make a commitment. Why can't she just be happy the way we are?"*

I believe that underneath men's aversion to commitment is plain, old-fashioned **fear of inadequacy**. At the heart of *"I don't want to make a commitment"* is the fear that we won't be able to please our partner forever, that we'll let her down somehow. I remember having thoughts about my being so much older than Francine and worrying that she might leave me for somebody who was younger and better looking. Luckily, instead of letting that get in the way, I trusted Francine's love for me and included her in my fears. If I hadn't, I might have found a way to sabotage the relationship in its infancy and we would never have had this glorious life together.

Commitment is freedom

Both men and women can be wary of the constraints commitment seems to impose. If we are reluctant to commit, often it's because we feel it will restrict us or somehow prevent us from expressing ourselves.

- *"I won't be able to have friends of the opposite sex."*
- *"I can't even look at another woman or she'll be jealous."*

- *"I won't be able to make my own decisions or do what I want."*
- *"I can't ever feel attracted to someone else again."*
- *"He'll get possessive and try to control me."*
- *"I'll lose my identity and have to give up my independence."*

We often think that commitment means **sacrificing something**, which immediately puts us in a state of deprivation. It's just like a diet—the more we won't let ourselves eat something, the more we want it. It's human nature to want what we think we can't have.

In fact, commitment sets us free. And why is that? How can making a life-long pact with one other person be freeing? Well, first of all, gone is the never-ending worry about whether **we** should stay or go—or whether **they'll** stay or go. Some friends of ours made a commitment early in their marriage that neither one of them would ever use divorce as a threat—the word is outlawed in their home. They agreed never to use that as ammunition against each other.

Another advantage of being committed is that we don't spend a lot of time worrying if we're with the right person every time our partner does something we don't like. Instead, we know they **are** the right person, and they did something we didn't like! Who wants to feel they're being judged and evaluated at every turn, that a scorecard is being tallied every day and they're running out of time? No wonder we get insecure in that kind of relationship! When we're committed, we don't have to pretend we're okay when we're not, so we don't drive our partner away. Instead, we put our attention on the real issue, namely:

"How do we resolve this and grow from it?"

When we know we are protected and honored inside the embrace of commitment, we can be fully ourselves. We don't have to monitor our behavior so we don't ruin the relationship. It's liberating to know that our partner is willing to go through a lifetime with us—that we're not contract employees, wondering when we're going to get laid off. When we are in a committed relationship, we're on staff—with full salary and all the benefits!

What harmony and bliss will come to us when we speak and hear the following words. What an experience—to no longer be afraid, to live in complete safety with another human being. We start with a declaration:

**"I'm committed to living with you,
learning with you, and loving you for
the rest of my life."**

Commitment is a gift

The environment of commitment provides a fertile soil in which we can become our true selves—the finest human beings we can be. When we are in a committed partnership, we are secure, buoyed and encircled by the love and respect of our partner. We're no longer alone— such happiness!

In the depths of our hearts, we know our partner is unconditionally committed to helping us fulfill our life purpose. When we are in the presence of commitment, we become the lucky recipients of one another's most empowering support.

But there is such a thing as genuine love, which is always considerate. Its distinguishing characteristic is,

in fact, regard for personal dignity. Its effect is to stimu-
late self-respect in the other person. Its concern is to
help the loved one to become their true self. Its purest
realization is its power to stimulate the other to attain
their highest self-realization.

Thus its effect is to draw the other out into freedom. And
if the loved one were called upon to give an account of
what that loved one had meant to them, they would say,
"I owe everything to it, most of all the fact that through
it I have become my real self."

—Romano Guardini

A Final Word

The purpose of this book is to offer you the opportunity to create the kind of relationships you've always wanted. We can give you the information and the tools, but the one thing we can't give you is **the willingness**. That is up to you and your partner. When we become willing to surrender ourselves to loving and being loved, to giving up our self-righteousness, to closing all the doors but the one that leads us home—we demonstrate human nature at its finest and offer our most sacred promise. In honoring the commitment to be in partnership, we apply our whole self to the process—one of the greatest privileges that will ever be bestowed upon us.

I promise if you make this commitment and continue to practice what you have discovered in this book, you'll know joy and peace unlike anything you've had before. Trust yourself and your love for one another, and find the courage to bring yourself forth even when you are the most afraid.

Imagine a world of committed partnerships—people honoring and taking care of one another, their families and communities. Think about how true partnership can provide so much of what is missing in the world. I see this in couples who trust that they are loved—they touch and inspire everyone they know.

We participate in the workings of the world every day. Let's treat each person that we are fortunate enough to encounter with dignity and respect. Commit your heart and your will to the practice of partnership. The more of us who are able to make that commitment, the closer we come to a world where each of us is safe.

We must not fall into cynicism or lose our faith in humanity. We are being called forth to live our lives with courage and purpose—especially in the face of the chaos around us. We live in challenging times, charged with the responsibility to live honestly and forthrightly within a society that tests us at every turn. Our success as a species rests on our ability to continually rise above that which keeps us small so that our planet becomes a sanctuary, not a battleground.

We can't change the world overnight, but we can change it in small increments—one person, one relationship at a time. Every time we do something honorable, it matters. Each moment we are alive, we have the option to treat one another with exquisite kindness, integrity, and compassion. We who are committed to healing ourselves and each other are the guardians of all that is good in the world, the protectors of our children, the emissaries of hope for humankind.

Our partnerships are the highest expression of our truest selves and contribute to everyone we are blessed to have in our lives. No matter where we are in our journey, we have been granted infinite opportunities to reclaim our birthright of safety and peace—and it begins with the original experience that unites us all: **trusting we are loved**.

Part Three

Exercises for Partnership

About the Exercises

What follows is a collection of simple exercises that will help you and your partner incorporate the concepts in this book into your own relationship. They serve as an introduction to some of the basic components of creating partnership in relationship, as well as a supportive framework that will guide you and your partner along your path. These exercises are designed to foster an environment of healthy communication, safety, and compassion—the ideal environment in which we can grow and heal.

Each of the ten practices for partnership has its own set of exercises, starting with an overview of essential information from each chapter. The exercises are set up in a linear fashion; however, it's important to remember that **listening with compassion** is at the heart of it all, running like an underground stream through every turn and bend of the journey. When we begin to communicate, breaking down the walls of silence, denial, and resentment, it is imperative that listening with compassion be our priority—remembering that our partners are giving us a gift by having the courage to speak their truth to us.

These exercises can be used in any of the following ways:

- On your own—either out loud into a tape recorder or written in a notebook.
- With your partner.
- With your partner in the presence of a counselor, therapist, or trusted friend.

Since one of the most important factors in any healing process is to become conscious of what may be going on beneath the surface, doing these exercises will assist you in gathering information which will help to increase your awareness about how you feel, what you fear, and where to focus your attention. When we have clarity about any given situation, we have much more ability to effect positive change. These exercises can bring you and your partner closer to what may be the source of your difficulties, making it easier to deal with the issues.

How to use these exercises

If your partner isn't ready or willing to do the exercises with you, or if you don't feel comfortable doing them with your partner at this time, that's okay. You may want to start working on them yourself, perhaps sharing insights as you go, or just keeping a journal. Many of the exercises involve making lists on your own, and others are comprised mainly of questions and answers, some of which can be adapted for an individual. Sometimes only one person will be interested in doing this kind of structured activity, and if this is the case, use these exercises as a way to take personal responsibility for yourself and your part in the relationship. **Any progress you make in**

your own growth process is going to contribute to the health of the relationship. If your partner doesn't choose to do this work with you at present, perhaps it is time for you to take it on yourself, demonstrating your commitment to the greater good. The exercises exist to support you and your partner—use them in whatever way seems appropriate.

How to get the most value out of the practices

Whether you do the exercises individually or as a couple, I recommend both of you get a good-sized notebook or journal specifically for this work. Read through the exercises before you begin. Some of them may excite or inspire you, others may seem confronting and bring up feelings of anxiety. This is normal—when we are about to move beyond our comfort zone, it is natural to feel some trepidation. However, this is an opportunity to demonstrate our courage and do it anyway! We must welcome these opportunities, realizing that the more challenging a particular exercise may be to do, the greater the potential is for healing. **These exercises will support the expansion of your ability to listen with compassion, apologize, forgive, speak from your heart, include one another, strengthen your commitment, create safety, and trust that you are loved.**

Another way to use the practices is to do them in the presence of a friend, counselor, or even another couple. If you and your partner have any concerns about what may come up for you as a result of doing these exercises, and this fear is keeping you from proceeding, then I would recommend enlisting the help of other people. Please don't allow your fears or concerns to stop you from moving forward. We've all avoided doing certain things because we imagined they might be painful, and that avoidance has cost us years of worry and precious energy. **Doing something is usually easier than resisting doing it.** Trust yourself and your partner—these exercises, done the way they are suggested, are designed to take care of you and keep you safe.

Note: Many of these exercises involve expressing emotions to your partner about specific situations in your relationship. Sometimes all that is required is that you and your partner hear one another with compassion. **If issues come up during any of the exercises that you want to explore further, communicate that clearly to your partner.** For instance, you might say, ***"I want to talk more about the upsets we have in regard to my health."*** Get your partner's alignment before launching into anything—don't assume that he or she is ready to discuss a certain situation until you have asked. If your partner does not feel ready to talk about a particular issue in that moment, respect his or her decision and make arrangements to do so at another time in the near future.

Making time to work on your partnership

To get the most benefit out of these exercises, attention must be paid to setting aside time specifically to work on them. Couples who carve out a schedule—without the interruptions of children or other distractions—find that their progress is accelerated dramatically. It will take time and commitment to sit down either with yourself or your partner and do these exercises, but that is where the majesty lies—**in our willingness to bring ourselves forth to honor**

ourselves and the one who loves us. The quality of our relationships affects our health, our work, our well-being. When we make creating partnership the highest priority, we take a stand that enhances the development of the other important areas of our lives.

Beginning the process

These practices represent a beginning—the doorway to a new way of listening and speaking. They serve as an introduction to the unfolding process of creating partnership and spending your life in an intimate union with another human being. Since the development of a relationship is not as linear as the exercises in this book, it is important to live inside a **paradigm of patience and forgiveness of yourself and your partner**. After reading this book and while working on the practices, you may discover that you are having significant breakthroughs, as well as feeling that you are "regressing," "stagnating," or "getting worse." Sometimes, uncovering long-buried communications and expressing the truth about how you feel can open up old wounds. This can often feel like you and your partner are losing ground—taking one step forward and two steps back—but this is normal and an essential part of the process. We need to remember how much we tend to be governed by what we think **should be happening**, when, in fact, **what is happening is exactly what needs to be happening**.

If you and your partner have long-standing issues or have not communicated well for many years, please try not to have unreasonable expectations about your progress. There is no easy fix, and it will take time to move through the pain to the joy and satisfaction that is available to you on the other side. Patience, forgiveness, and an atmosphere of compassion must be consciously cultivated. **When we find ourselves invalidating the situation or being critical of ourselves or our partner, we must strive to bring ourselves back to our commitment to the process.** As you and your partner move through these exercises, remember: **no matter what is said or how it is said, your partner loves you.** Every communication is a gift. Every situation has a lesson within it, and every moment we are alive is another opportunity to **trust that we are loved.**

How to listen with compassion

- Keep your complete focus on the other person.
- Let your partner talk at first without interrupting. If they hesitate, ask encouraging questions such as ***"Is there anything else?" "Is there more?"*** If your attention wanders to your own thoughts, move it back to them as soon as you notice.
- Be genuinely interested—find out what they're really thinking and feeling.
- If it's appropriate, ask questions which will help you more fully understand what's going on with them.
- Imagine what it would be like to **be** them, having their emotions and experiences.
- Remember, even if they're complaining about you, they're always speaking about **their own pain.**
- Notice if you have a need to judge, defend, justify, explain, or criticize. Let these reactions

go and put your attention back on your loved
one. You'll have a chance to communicate.
Be patient.

- Validate or recreate (reflect back) their feelings
  and statements when appropriate.

- Notice if you have a desire to give advice, offer
  help, make suggestions—but don't do it yet.
  There will be time for all of that later. Right now,
  your job is to **listen**.

- Listen the way you want them to listen to you.

- Remember that you are loved, and welcome their
  communication as a gift and an opportunity for
  growth. If they are upset with you, remember the
  mantras... *"She loves me... He loves me..."*

Setting up the Listening

The Compassion Process

The process that follows was developed to create a
safe environment so that you and your partner can say
whatever you need to say, and be heard with compassion.
You can use this exercise whenever you feel afraid to
communicate, and it will help generate a compassionate,
loving atmosphere between you and your partner. Once
this environment is created, you will find that even previ-
ously taboo subjects can be discussed more easily in the
spirit of partnership.

Instructions: Sit with your partner. The person who
wishes to speak first reads each item from the **Speaker**
list. Make eye contact with your partner as much as possible. It helps to read each sentence first, digest it for a

moment, and then say it. Your partner does not need to respond verbally to these statements.

After you have completed the **Speaker** part, your partner then reads from the **Listener** part. Once this is complete, the speaker can then deliver the communication. Exchange roles if necessary. After a while, you may find that certain phrases from these lists resonate for you, and you can simply say them to remind your partner to listen with compassion without having to go through the entire structured process.

Speaker

There are some things I need to say to you.
I haven't said them because I've been afraid.

I've been afraid that you won't
listen to me with compassion—
afraid you will judge me, or get upset,
or not honor my feelings exactly the way they are.

I have withheld my communication, and experienced
the pain of holding back a part of myself from you.

I apologize for withholding myself from you.
I realize that doing so eventually causes more pain,
and dishonors our relationship.

I apologize for not trusting that you love me. I apologize
for any pain I have caused you by not communicating.

When I say what I need to say, please listen that
I love you, and that I am committed to our relationship.

Please hear what I say as an essential part
of our healing process.

Sharing my whole self is a gift I give to you.
I trust you with my heart.

Thank you for making it safe for me to speak,
and thank you for loving me.

Listener

Thank you for being willing to communicate
what you have been afraid to say.

I apologize for having not made it
safe for you to communicate.
I apologize for forgetting that you love me.

I am sorry for the pain you have experienced
by holding yourself back.

I apologize for the times I have judged you, or not
listened to you, or invalidated your feelings.

I have been afraid to hear your withholds, but I realize
that not listening to them eventually causes
more pain, and dishonors our relationship.

I will make it safe for you to share your whole
self with me. I will listen that you love me.
I will listen with compassion.

I am committed to our relationship.
I will hear whatever you say
as an essential part of our healing process.

I will accept your communications as a gift.
Thank you for trusting me with your heart.

I love you. Thank you for loving me.

Please, tell me what you have been afraid to say.

**Note: Ask your partner if what he or she wants is
simply to be heard, or if he or she wants to engage in
a conversation about the issues. Don't assume that
you have permission to discuss their communication.
If your partner just wants you to listen with compassion and not go any further, please honor that and
set up a time to talk about it together later.**

CHAPTER 1

Trusting You Are Loved

If you want to honor the people you love,
let them love you.

You always have been, and always will be loved—
you don't have to get love, you already have it.

When we were very young, we forgot we were loved.
It's as simple and as complicated as that.

We hurt our loved ones when
we don't let them love us.

When we listen we are loved, **we hear what's being said.**
When we don't listen we are loved, **we hear
more evidence that we are not loved.**

Trusting we are loved begins with the
declaration we make to ourselves:
I AM LOVED.

Your parents love(d) you.
Your partner loves you.

Become aware of what causes you to forget you are loved.
Give up the need to be loved a certain way.

Trusting we are loved happens in the present moment.

It is an experience that gets stronger over time.
We will always forget we are loved—the majesty
of human beings is that we can always remember.

Exercises

1. Most of us have unconscious mental lists to determine whether or not we are loved. We're not generally aware of the criteria we use, but we usually know when we feel loved or not. We've all developed a set of rules and regulations by which we measure the love in our lives—some of them are more rigid than others, depending on our level of trust. The purpose of this exercise is to help us become aware of our own list and our partner's, and begin to see it for what it is—a set of standards that may or may not be the truth. Take out your notebook and write the following headings, using a separate page for each. Then begin making your lists.

- *If _____ really loved me, (s)he would:*

- *If _____ really loved me, (s)he wouldn't:*

Write down everything that comes to you—don't censor or edit, no matter how unrealistic or outrageous it may seem. You may have ten items or one hundred. When you can't think of any more, share them with your partner. You don't have to do anything specific with this information. Discussion may be appropriate, but not necessary. The important thing is to become more aware of what you and your partner believe love needs to look like.

2. Sit across from your partner and make the following requests of each other. After each answer, the suggested response is: *"Thank you"* or *"Thank you for including me."* These questions will help you gather more information about your own and your partner's experience of trusting you are loved.

As with all of the exercises, allow your partner to

continue speaking as long as he or she wants. If your partner hesitates but doesn't appear finished, ask the question again or **"Is there more?"** or **"Is there anything else?"** When the first person feels that everything has been communicated, then exchange roles.

- *Please tell me when you don't trust that I love you*

- *Please tell me when you trust that I love you*

- *Please tell me what triggers you to forget that I love you*

- *Please tell me what has you remember that I love you*

- *Please tell me how I can help you trust that you are loved*

- *Please tell me how you feel I do not let myself be loved*

- *Please tell me in what instances you would like me to let myself be loved*

3. When you have finished that sequence, speak the following statements to your partner. Suggested responses are: **"Thank you"** or **"I forgive you,"** *and* **"You're welcome."** Exchange roles.

- *I apologize for the pain I have caused you when I don't let you love me*

- *I apologize for the pain I have caused you when I don't trust that I am loved*

- *Thank you for loving me*

- *Thank you for letting me love you*

CHAPTER 2

Listening with Compassion

When we are heard, we are healed.

Compassion is a very deep appreciation of another
person's feelings and experience.

Compassion is not: feeling sorry for, relating to,
identifying with, or agreeing. It is not judgment,
evaluation, giving advice, helping, or analyzing.
In compassion we simply hear
what is being said to us.

When we listen with compassion, everything
we say or do will be appropriate.

Compassion must be created—it comes from a choice
to take our attention off **ourselves** and be
of genuine service to another person.

When we validate (or recreate) someone's experience,
their pain lessens or disappears.
When we invalidate or resist someone's
experience, their pain intensifies.

We cannot be afraid of anyone for whom we
have compassion. Listen with compassion and
trust that you are loved.

Exercises

1. Sit with your partner and ask each other the following questions. Suggested responses to the answers are acknowledging statements such as *"Thank you,"* *"I hear you,"* *"That makes sense,"* *"I'm sorry,"* or whatever feels appropriate. Ask *"Is there anything else?"* or *"Is there more?"* when necessary. Exchange roles.

- *In our life together, what is easy for you to have compassion for?*

- *In our life together, what is difficult for you to have compassion for?*

- *What would you like me to have more compassion for in our relationship?*

- *What would you like to have more compassion for in our relationship?*

2. After you have completed the questions, make the following statements to your partner. Suggested responses are *"Thank you,"* or *"I forgive you."*

- *I apologize for the pain I cause you when I do not have compassion for* _____ (fill in appropriate situation, repeat as necessary).

- *I apologize for the pain I caused you when I did not have compassion for* _____ (fill in appropriate instance, repeat).

- *Thank you for having compassion for* _____ (*"You're welcome"*—repeat as necessary).

CHAPTER 3

Apology

> Apology is not an admission of guilt,
> it is an act of love.
>
> Apology is a compassionate statement that says we are
> willing to take responsibility for the consequences
> of our actions and to make someone else's feelings more
> important than our desire to be right.
>
> When we apologize, we are not being called upon to pass
> judgment about what happened—we are simply
> acknowledging that something we
> did or didn't do affected another person.
>
> The more specific we make our
> apology, the more power it has.
>
> Apology is not an admission of failure
> or weakness—it is an act of courage.

The Three Basic Apologies

- *"I'm sorry you're upset."*

- *"I'm sorry you're upset and if I had anything to do with it, I apologize."*

- *"I'm sorry I upset you and I apologize."*

Exercise

1. Ask your partner the question: *"Please tell me what you would like me to apologize for."* Your partner will answer with: *"I would like you to apologize for _____ ."* Continue this until he or she has no further requests. After each request, apologize without explanation or justification. Once the apology is made, the suggested response is: *"Thank you"* or *"I forgive you."* For the purposes of this exercise, stay with simple apologies such as:

- *I'm sorry for _____ .*
- *I apologize for _____ .*
- *I'm sorry I upset you.*
- *I'm sorry I hurt you.*
- *I apologize for the pain I caused you.*
- *I apologize for hurting you.*

Note: If you are moved to apologize more specifically, or if your partner needs a more extensive apology to experience being heard or taken care of, please feel free to do so.

CHAPTER 4

Forgiveness

Forgiveness is a gift we give ourselves.

Forgiveness is the cornerstone of partnership.
When we forgive, we renounce anger or resentment
against another, and give up the need to punish.

Forgiving does not mean we condone
or excuse the deed, but we can appreciate
why it may have been done.

Compassion is at the heart of forgiveness.

Apology and forgiveness are partners. When we
are accountable for our actions, it is much
easier to be forgiven.

There is magic in
speaking the words *"I forgive you"*

When we forgive, we liberate
ourselves from suffering.

Be kinder than you think is necessary.

Exercises

1. Make these lists in your notebook, using a page for
each heading. After your lists are complete, share each
item with your partner. Then exchange roles. The

suggested responses are: *"Thank you,"* or *"Thank you for telling me,"* or *"I'm sorry."*

- *Things I haven't forgiven myself for* (include things in your relationship with your partner as well as other areas of your life)

- *Things I haven't forgiven you* (your partner) *for*

- *Things I want to forgive myself for*

- *Things I want to forgive you* (your partner) *for*

- *Things I feel you haven't forgiven me for*

- *Things I am not ready or willing to forgive* (things regarding your partner, yourself, or other areas of your life)

2. Using both of your lists as references, sit with your partner and make the following requests and statements. When you have gone through the entire sequence, exchange roles.

- *Please forgive me for* _____ . (Your partner's suggested response is *"I forgive you."* Repeat the statement for each item.)

- *I forgive you for* _____ (respond with *"Thank you"*—repeat statement as necessary).

- *I forgive myself for* _____ (respond with *"Thank you"*—repeat).

NOTE: If during this process your partner asks you to forgive them and you do not feel ready to, first ask yourself: *"What am I holding onto? Is it worth the cost to not forgive?"* Perhaps you feel your partner should apologize, or, if he or she has already done so, perhaps the apology needs to be delivered in a different way. If you still aren't able to forgive even after your partner apologizes, then tell the truth and say, ***"I want to forgive you, and I'm not ready yet. Please have compassion for me."*** There is tremendous power in simply saying what is true for us in the moment—when we speak from our hearts, we give ourselves room to move on. You may find yourself being willing to forgive the moment after you communicate your unwillingness. If you are not willing to forgive, that's okay. This is a process. Strive to reach beyond your comfort zone and forgive, but also trust that you will when it is appropriate.

CHAPTER 5

Speaking from Your Heart

When we speak from our heart, we always tell the truth.

Answer questions and acknowledge statements.
We don't need to justify, explain, or embellish
why we feel the way we do.

Let go of the need to blame your partner for why you have
been afraid to speak from your heart.

Notice when you are writing the script ahead of time
and making it real—instead of believing your inner
conversation, find out what's really happening with
your partner.

Being honest doesn't mean being brutal—avoid accusatory
speaking. Begin with *"I am..."* instead of *"You are..."*

Speaking from the heart becomes much easier
when we trust that we are loved.

Exercise

1. Using a page for each heading, make the following lists in your notebook, then share them with your partner. **Listen with compassion to each other.** After your partner says each item, say *"Thank you,"* or *"Thank you for including me,"* or *"I'm sorry you've been afraid (or ashamed)":*

- *Things I've made up about why I can't tell you the truth*

- *Things I haven't been telling the truth about*

- *Things I've done that I'm afraid or ashamed to tell you*

- *Things I've not done that I'm afraid or ashamed to tell you*

- *Thoughts I've had that I'm afraid or ashamed to tell you*

- *Feelings I'm having that I'm afraid or ashamed to tell you*

- *Ways I am judging you that I'm afraid or ashamed to tell you*

- *Things I'm disappointed about that I'm afraid or ashamed to tell you*

- *Ways I have misrepresented you to others that I'm afraid or ashamed to tell you*

Note: Some of these communications may be difficult to deliver and/or to hear. Telling the truth is essential if we want our relationships to move forward. Please remember that you are loved, and please listen with compassion. Make it safe for your partner to speak from their heart.

CHAPTER 6

Creating Safety

An appropriate human being is one
in whose presence we are safe.

Being safe is one of the most basic needs of human
beings—it's even more basic than feeling loved.

The first step to creating safety is to face the fact that we
are all afraid. We only cause harm to others when
we ourselves feel threatened.

Fear wears three masks: judgment, anger, and withdrawal.
Strive to express fear appropriately
as soon as you are aware of it.

Our first priority is **to make it safe for others**.
When we create safety for others, we will be safe.

Courage is not the absence of fear.
Courage is being afraid and doing it anyway.

Take the stand and declare your intention:

I will make him safe in my presence.

I will make her safe in my presence.

Exercises

1. Use the following questions to increase your awareness about creating safety. In your notebooks, write down the following questions and your answers. Most of these won't take more than a few words or sentences. When you are complete, begin a conversation by sharing your answers with your partner.

- *Do I feel safe with my partner?*
- *Do I feel safe in my family?*
- *Do I feel safe at my job?*
- *Whom do I feel safe with?*
- *What does this person (or people) do that has made me feel safe?*
- *Whom do I feel unsafe with?*
- *What does this person (or people) do that has made me feel unsafe?*
- *What would have me feel safer in my life/home/job?*
- *Who in my life feels safe with me?*
- *What do I do that has this person(s) feel safe?*
- *Who may feel unsafe with me?*
- *What do I do that has this person(s) feel unsafe?*
- *What can I do to have people feel safer in my presence?*

2. With your partner, take turns making the following requests and responding to the answers with **"Thank you,"** or **"Thank you for telling me."** Then exchange roles. When you have gone through the entire sequence together, declare your commitment to creating safety.

- *Please tell me when you feel safe with me.*

- *Please tell me when you feel unsafe.*

- *Please tell me what I can do to have you feel safer with me.*

- *Please tell me what you need from me when you are* _____ *(upset) (angry) (frightened) (worried).* Ask separately for each emotion.

Declaration:

I am committed to creating safety for you.
Thank you for being committed to creating safety for me.

CHAPTER 7

Creating Intimacy:
Include Your Partner

Trust creates intimacy, intimacy creates trust.
When we trust, we will be trusted.
When we include others, they will include us.

Intimacy is the natural result of creating safety.

We are afraid to include our partners
because we don't trust that we are loved.

All of us have been hurt and betrayed at
some point when we've opened our hearts. It's time
to acknowledge we've been holding back and ask
ourselves this question:

***"Am I willing to give up everything I think I know for the
possibility of what could be?"***

Relationships usually don't die because of what's said—
they die because of what's **not** said.

Include your partner as soon as you know of something
that will affect them or possibly upset them.

Include your partner even if your plans, thoughts,
or ideas aren't fully realized.

Create trust by saying what you have been unwilling
to say—in the act of communicating, we
create trusting we are loved.

Exercise

1. Make the following headings in your notebook, leaving an entire page for each list. When you have finished, sit with your partner and communicate each item. The suggested responses can be any of the following, or whatever feels right: *"Thank you," "Thank you for telling me," "Thank you for including me," "Thank you for trusting me,"* or *"I'm sorry."* Some of the headings may seem similar to some of the ones in the exercises for **Speaking from Your Heart**, but you will find that different things will come up for you. Even if some of what comes up is similar, it is still important to communicate it again in this context. These lists will probably cover just about everything that you may be withholding from your partner and even yourself. **Please remember to listen with compassion** and make it safe for your partner to include you in this intimate way.

- *Thoughts I haven't been sharing with you*

- *Feelings I haven't been sharing with you*

- *Ideas I haven't been sharing with you*

- *Desires I haven't been sharing with you*

- *Fears I haven't been sharing with you*

- *Things I have been avoiding saying to you*

- *Broken agreements with myself that I haven't communicated to you*

- *Broken agreements with you that I haven't communicated to you*

- *Things I'm judging myself about that I haven't communicated to you*

- *Things I'm judging you about that I haven't communicated to you*

- *Things I've been putting off that I've said I would do*

- *Things you've asked me to do that I have not done*

- *Well-being issues that I am not taking care of:* (Financial/Physical/Emotional/Spiritual—*Make a separate list for each*)

CHAPTER 8

Handling Upsets Responsibly

Upsets are nature's way of telling us
attention must be paid.

Being upset is a normal part of the human condition but
one that we consistently invalidate. Our culture
is based on looking good and being happy.

Upsets focus our vision on what needs to be
healed—they are a pathway to sanity and
wholeness and not to be feared.

Upsets are usually caused by
wanting things and people to be different
from the way they are, or because we or our partner are
holding back from one another.

When we are not trusting we are loved, not listening
with compassion, or adding meaning to
a situation, we often get upset.

To receive the gifts upsets hold for us,
we must be willing to let go of our self-righteousness and
make getting back into partnership
our highest priority.

The measure of a healthy relationship
is not whether upsets occur, but rather how quickly
we can recover and learn the lessons they
have to teach us.

Trust that you are loved.

How to handle upsets responsibly:

- Speak from your heart
- Listen with compassion
- Apologize
- Forgive
- Give up self-righteousness

Exercise

1. In your notebook, make the following lists. Share each item with your partner. Suggested responses are: *"Thank you," "Thank you for including me," "I'm sorry you're so hard on yourself,"* or *"I forgive you."*

- *Things I say to myself when I am upset*
- *Things I want to say to you when I am upset*
- *Recurring upsets in my relationship with you*
- *What I've been expecting and getting disappointed about*
- *What I've been unwilling to say in regard to being upset*
- *What I've made it mean when you* _____
- *Ways I try to avoid upsetting you*
- *Ways I try to avoid getting upset*
- *Ways I blame myself for upsets*
- *Ways I blame you for upsets*

- *Ways I would like to be when I am upset*

- *Ways I would like you to be when you are upset*

Note: Remember—if issues come up during this exercise that you want to explore further, express that clearly to your partner. If your partner does not feel ready to talk about a particular issue, ask for another time in the near future when you can both agree to sit down and look at it together.

CHAPTER 9

Expressing Appreciation

The greatest gift we can give humankind
is to love and let ourselves be loved.

We have a need to know we matter. We need
to live in the experience that we are known,
honored, noticed, important,
valued, and cherished.

We need to do more than **feel** our appreciation for
someone—we need to **speak** it. Each time we do,
it makes a difference.

When we appreciate people, we do much more
than validate them—we help them create their
experience of themselves. We can either stifle or
support one another by our perceptions.

When we cannot accept another's acknowledgment,
we dishonor their experience of us.

We contribute to others when we
allow them to contribute to us.

Although we naturally notice
what's not working, we must train ourselves to
see what **is** working and express it.

Remember the words of Aesop:
***"Kindness has power when strength
and force often fail."***

Exercises

1. Leave a full page in your notebooks and make the following lists. Follow the same procedure as in the other exercises you do with your partner. The suggested response to each item is indicated:

- *Things I want to thank you for* *("You're welcome")*

- *Things I have thanked you for but want to thank you again* *("You're welcome")*

- *Things I have overlooked or forgotten to thank you for* *("You're welcome")*

- *What I appreciate about you* *("Thank you"—* Repeat often)

- *What I appreciate about our relationship* *("Thank you")*

- *Things I want you to thank me for* *("Thank you for _____")*

- *Things I want to be acknowledged for* *("I acknowledge you for _____")*

- *Things I haven't felt acknowledged or appreciated for* *("I'm sorry," or "I apologize")*

- *I feel loved and taken care of when you _____* *("Thank you for telling me")*

- *The things I admire about you are _____ .*

2. Write a love letter to your partner on beautiful stationery. Speak from your heart and express your appreciation voluminously—go on and on about how wonderful they are, how much you adore them, how important they are to you. Really gush—saturate them with your love, and don't hold back anything! Make a date to go out to your favorite restaurant and then give each other the letters to read.

3. Each day, during dinner at home or before bed, ask this question of one another. Spend about ten minutes or so on each person:

- *Please tell me what you would like to be acknowledged for* or *Please tell me how you would like to be appreciated.*

After your partner feels fully appreciated, then offer them your own heart-felt thanks about whatever you wish:

- *I would also like to acknowledge you for* _____ .

CHAPTER 10

Honoring Your Commitment

When we think *"I don't want to commit until I'm sure it will work,"* we've got it backwards.

Commitment is a leap of faith.
We commit without a guarantee.
In the act of committing, we create
the security and safety that we seek.

Until we are committed, each conflict calls the relationship into question. When we are committed, we are safe. Whatever comes up is just the next thing to deal with, not something to be resisted or feared.

Taking a vow isn't always enough. When the obstacles arise, we must sometimes re-commit again and again. Commitment needs to be nurtured, demonstrated, and strengthened over time.

Commitment frees us. Gone is the fear of being abandoned—we are able to turn our energies to the task at hand.

When we are committed, the question
"Are you the right person?" has no more power over us.
The question we live with becomes:
"How can we resolve this and grow from it?"

Exercises

1. If possible, go to the place where you first made your commitment to one another. If that isn't feasible, go where you both have good memories about your relationship and where you'd feel safe to express emotion.

- **Talk about when you first fell in love with one another, and what it was about each other that had you know you'd found your life partner. Share how it felt to make that initial commitment as a way of re-connecting to the essence of your relationship.**

2. Ask the following questions of one another and allow the conversation to unfold and evolve:

- *What are you committed to regarding yourself?*
- *What are you committed to regarding me?*
- *What are you committed to regarding our relationship?*

The Commitment Declaration

The following is a powerful expression of commitment. **Instructions:** You say each item in **Part I** while your partner listens. Take your time and try to keep eye contact as much as possible. Your partner need not say anything in response unless they are moved to do so. When you have completed **Part I**, your partner will then say each item in **Part II**. Then exchange roles. When you are finished, each of you will have had the opportunity to speak your commitment and thank your partner for theirs. You can use this process as a way of setting the context for your journey towards partnership, or whenever you feel it necessary to declare your commitment to your relationship.

Part I

_____ (name), I am committed to you
and our relationship.
I will not give up on you.
I will not give up on us.
I freely choose you as my partner.
I will view everything that happens as an
opportunity to grow.
I will see you as the embodiment
of all that is good in the world.
I will use you as a mirror to see
exactly how I need to heal.
I will do whatever I can to support
your success and happiness.
I will trust that you love me.
I will listen to you with compassion.
I will apologize to you when I upset you, either
intentionally or unintentionally.
I will forgive you.
I will tell you the truth and include you.
I will speak from my heart.
I will make it safe for you.
I will honor and respect our differences.
I will see all our upsets as doorways to healing.
I will acknowledge and appreciate you.
I will honor our commitment.
I will let you love me.
I will always love you.

Part II

_____ name), thank you for being
committed to me and to our relationship.
Thank you for not giving up on me.
Thank you for not giving up on us.
Thank you for freely choosing me as your partner.
Thank you for viewing everything that happens
as an opportunity to grow.
Thank you for seeing me as the embodiment
of all that is good in the world.
Thank you for using me as a mirror to see
exactly how you need to heal.
Thank you for doing whatever you can to
support my success and happiness.
Thank you for trusting that I love you.
Thank you for listening to me with compassion.
Thank you for apologizing to me when you upset me,
either intentionally or unintentionally.
Thank you for forgiving me.
Thank you for telling me the truth and including me.
Thank you for speaking from your heart.
Thank you for making it safe for me.
Thank you for honoring and respecting our differences.
Thank you for seeing all our upsets
as doorways to healing.
Thank you for acknowledging and appreciating me.
Thank you for honoring our commitment.
Thank you for letting me love you.
I will always love you.

Congratulations! And please remember—go easy on yourself and your partner as you embark upon creating partnership in relationship. Trust the process! It took some time for you to get to where you are now. Don't get caught up in the desire to rush, or get too discouraged if some of the practices are challenging or the concepts don't become second nature overnight. Every small step we make in our willingness to grow makes a difference— change isn't always measured in quantum leaps. In fact, the most lasting healing is the kind we do gradually, over time, in small increments. Give yourself and your partner permission to explore this work at your own pace, in an atmosphere of safety and compassion. Thank you for your commitment to one another, and thank you for **trusting you are loved.**

About the Authors
Lew Epstein / Francine Epstein

Born in 1919 in Bridgeport, Connecticut to poor Russian immigrants, Lew's family moved to New York City when he was six months old. As the second youngest of five children, he grew up and came of age on the impoverished streets of the Lower East Side of Manhattan. As a young man, Lew was a journalist, a political activist, an actor, and an entertainer.

In 1943, Lew married artist Norma Scheff, had three children, and became a successful entertainer and public speaker. That marriage ended after 26 years.

In 1973, Lew married Francine and they have been partners for twenty-five years. Francine was born in 1944 and grew up in Queens, NY. She has one daughter, Marci, from her previous marriage.

Lew and Francine participated in various self-awareness courses and workshops beginning with the *est* Training in 1973. The combination of their experiences in this work and in their own relationship, along with Lew's already extensive knowledge of the teachings of contemporary philosophers, became the springboard for Lew and Francine to develop their own innate wisdom in the area of human relationships.

Since 1983, Lew and Francine have been leading their Men's and Women's Clubs in several cities in the United States and Europe. At these monthly meetings, men and women gather to discuss and practice what it takes to have relationships work.

The principles found in this book are those that have been introduced and practiced in the Clubs, workshops, retreats, and conferences Lew and Francine have been leading together for over fifteen years, including *The Couples' Day* and *The Couples' Retreat*.

Francine is now also bringing this work of creating partnership into corporations.

Lew and Francine Epstein live in the San Francisco Bay Area.

Reppy Epstein Kirkilis

Reppy was born in New York City in 1952, one of Lew and Norma Epstein's three children. She has two brothers, Jonathan and Kenny.

With a similar background in self-awareness training and philosophies as her father, Reppy has been a relationship coach since 1987, counseling couples and families. The work of Lew and Francine Epstein has been instrumental in her development as a relationship consultant.

Reppy is also a professional writer, illustrator, and entertainer, producing theatrical events and publishing artistic works since 1973. Her most recent project prior to writing this book was the December 1996 release of her first CD, *Legacy*, a collection of original piano solos from 1976-1995.

Reppy has been married to John Kirkilis since 1983. John and Reppy have a daughter, Alexandra, and live in central Texas.

About The Partnership Foundation

A close friend of mine brought me to Lew Epstein's Men's Club in 1988. I was surprised and moved at how these men—accomplished, healthy, and in control—when actually given the opportunity to share themselves authentically, expressed the depth of the love and pain they felt on a daily basis, particularly for their wives and children.

I learned a great deal about the power of compassionate listening, and Lew's "simple, but not easy" practices for cultivating a strong, fulfilling intimate relationship. Through Lew, Francine, and the Club members' support and inspiration, I sought out, found, and married my own life partner in 1996.

For over 15 years, in Men's, Women's, and Combined Clubs meeting monthly in 6 cities in the United States and England, Lew and Francine created safe havens for hundreds of people to openly discuss their lives and their personal relationships. By sharing the joys and struggles they faced in their own marriage, and by reasserting time and again the priceless gift that an intimate relationship is, Lew and Francine inspired the Club members to create, nurture, and value their own partnerships.

When Lew and Francine announced their retirement from the annual Internationals (all-Club conferences), two participants, Charlie Smith and Nestor Figueroa, stepped forward to ensure that this important work would continue to be given to the world. They formed a not-for-profit organization that came to be called The Partnership Foundation.

From those years of powerful and heartfelt conversations within the Clubs, there emerged the ten Practices for Partnership illustrated in this book. The Partnership

Foundation offers programs, conferences, videos, audio tapes, and open dialogues that continue the ongoing evolution of these practices. We are very proud to be the publishers of this book; it is Lew Epstein's legacy and has become our source manual.

We believe these practices are so fundamental to human relationships and are so much in harmony with our hearts, that they cross all borders of race, gender, sexual preference, religion, age and culture. We are committed to people being able to create true, vibrant partnerships. Cooperation is something humanity greatly needs, especially now when our very survival and the health of the planet are at stake. This book, and the work of The Partnership Foundation, can show us which steps to take to start a life's journey of compassion and love for one another.

If you would like to be part of our vision of a world based on Partnership in Relationship—a world where everyone is safe—please contact us via our web site or address on the next page.

Our thanks go to Lew and Francine, and Lew's daughter Reppy, for their magnificent hearts, their compassion for people, and their inspiration to all of us to live a life of partnership.

Tom Herndon
Executive Director
The Partnership Foundation

To order additional copies of *Trusting You Are Loved—Practices for Partnership,* and for information on speaking engagements, audio tapes, and workshops, please contact The Partnership Foundation. Quantity discounts are available.

The Partnership Foundation
775 E. Blithedale #106
Mill Valley, CA 94941
Phone: (415) 458-1945
email: tpfmail@aol.com

VISIT OUR WEB SITE!
www.partnership.org